Valuing Ourselves as We Grow Older

Explorations of Meaning and Purpose

AGING WITH FINESSE, BOOK 1

MARY L. FLETT, PHD

Five Pillars of Aging Press

Sonoma, California

Copyright © 2021 by **Mary L. Flett, PhD**

All rights reserved. No part of this publication may be reproduced, distributed or transmitted in any form or by any means, without prior written permission. Published in the United States by:

Five Pillars of Aging Press	Five Pillars of Aging Press
P.O. Box 134	157 Temelec Circle
El Verano, CA 95433	Sonoma, CA 95476

https://fivepillarsofaging.com
Five Pillars of Aging Press First Edition, 2021
First Printing
Cover Design: Jessica Reed

THE POEMS OF EMILY DICKINSON: VARIORUM EDITION, edited by Ralph W. Franklin, Cambridge, Mass.: The Belknap Press of Harvard University Press, Copyright © 1998 by the President and Fellows of Harvard College. Copyright ©1951, 1955 by the President and Fellows of Harvard College. Copyright © renewed 1979, 1983 by the President and Fellows of Harvard College. Copyright © 1914, 1918, 1919, 1924, 1929, 1930, 1932, 1935, 1937, 1942 by Martha Dickinson Bianchi. Copyright © 1952, 1957, 1958, 1963, 1965 by Mary L. Hampson.

Unless otherwise credited, poems courtesy of Carol Mikoda

Although this publication is designed to provide accurate information in regard to the subject matter covered, the publisher and the author assume no responsibility for errors, inaccuracies, omissions, or any other inconsistencies herein. This publication is meant as a source of valuable information for the reader, however it is not meant as a replacement for direct expert assistance. If such level of assistance is required, the services of a competent professional should be sought. Unless otherwise indicated, all the characters in this book are fictitious. Any resemblance to actual persons, living or dead, is purely coincidental.

Book Layout © 2017 BookDesignTemplates.com
Valuing Ourselves as we Grow Older. -- 1st ed.
ISBN: 978-1-7342359-5-3

This book is dedicated to my maternal grandfather,

Edward Arden Sipp

All the striving is over now. We don't have to prove ourselves anymore. We don't have to have the way we spend our time approved anymore. We don't have to work, produce, provide, or get ahead anymore. The only thing required of us now is the blooming of the self. Like autumn flowers, rich in color, deep in tone, sturdy in the wind, our lives not only have new color, they bring with them the kind of interior depth a fast-moving world so dearly needs.

—*Joan Chittister*

Contents

Preface i

Acknowledgments iii

PURPOSE & MEANING AS WE AGE 1

GIVING AND RECEIVING 7

GRATITUDE 13

THREE LOSSES 19

BECAUSE I COULD NOT STOP FOR DEATH 25

HAPPY BIRTHDAY, MOM! 31

WAITING 37

GENERATION GAPS 43

LEFT BEHIND 49

FINDING PURPOSE AND MEANING IN A PANDEMIC 55

LET THERE BE LIGHT 61

NEEDING A LULLABY TO SOOTHE ME 67

TO EVERY THING THERE IS A SEASON 73

PAUSING FOR A MOMENT 79

SANCTUARY 85

THE IMPORTANCE OF LEAVING A LEGACY OF VALUES	91
LEGACY OF PROTEST	97
PASSING THE BATON	103
GATES	109
THIS WEEK IN HISTORY	115
STAYING CONNECTED IN OUR SEPARATENESS	121
PERSONAL VALUES	127
ONCE UPON A TIME . . .	133
Resources	139

Preface

I STARTED WRITING A WEEKLY blog in November, 2017 for the Center for Aging and Values. This was my opportunity to explore issues that have essential importance to me as an aging adult and, at that time, to my patients. Since then, I have published a blog every Sunday including several guest blogs and a couple of reprints of blogs I thought had "legs".

In 2020, faced with the consequences of COVID, I decided to pull my blogs together and publish them in book format. This journey has resulted in the Aging with Finesse series, of which this is the first book. Contents differ slightly from the original postings (and are much improved) due of the excellent editorial eye of Cathy Cambron.

Book 1 in this series is centered on the importance of values in my life. The study of values seems to have an ebb and flow. Values were the focus of my dissertation in the late 1990s but fell out of fashion in the early years of the century. As this book and others in the Aging with Finesse series are published, the study of values is returning to focus because of a shift in consciousness.

Values are a difficult topic to pin down because they have so many different facets. There are moral values and personal values and cultural and social values. When asked to name your values, you might actually have difficulty doing so without an example. Even if you are clear about your values, explaining where they came from and how they inform your day-to-day life is often fraught with vagueness.

In this book I explore different aspects of my values within the context of contemporary events. Along with the original publication date, I have added author's notes to bookmark historical events that were clear and impactful when I wrote about them but now have retreated to history and decreased in importance with the passing of time and their replacement by other, sometimes more outrageous incidents.

My hope is that you find yourself in the writing and are validated in your own self-worth. I also hope you come across unexpected and different ways of valuing yourself that offer new insights into how you are aging.

Acknowledgments

SCATTERED THROUGHOUT THIS BOOK ARE poems by my dear friend Carol Mikoda. Carol is an extraordinarily gifted poet, as well as a bon vivant, a musician, a mother, a professor, and an old soul whom I have delighted in knowing and calling my friend for close to half a century. She has kindly permitted me to use her words to make mine better.

This series of books would not have come to see the light of day without the support and encouragement of Hillevi Ruumet, who lent me her eagle eye for proofreading and who spent countless hours in conversation with me pondering purpose and meaning. She continues to add value and meaning to my life.

I also have deep gratitude for the support of Ruth Schwartz and her far-reaching network of experts who helped me launch these words into the world of self-publishing.

Finally, I thank the core readers of my blog, who over the past four years have provided me with validation and inspiration to share my observations and insights on valuing ourselves as we grow older.

PURPOSE & MEANING AS WE AGE

Originally published July 8, 2018

ONE OF THE MOST FREQUENT *refrains I hear from my patients is that they no longer have purpose in their lives. Many are coming to see me because they are experiencing sadness, hopelessness, and a loss of direction. It is obvious to me that they are struggling with their identity, their usefulness, and the context for who they are now. Finding purpose at any age can be a challenging task. It is especially challenging when society no longer has a place for you.*

Defining Purpose

THE ADDED SPICE IN LIFE that helps bridge the gaps of boredom, meaninglessness, empty repetition, and pain is purpose. It is what brings meaning to what you do, gives you a sense of accomplishment in developing mastery or skill, and sustains you in challenging times. Informed by your beliefs, values, and habits, purpose can slowly change over time or shift in an instant. Purpose may consist of step-by-step instructions with an attainable goal at the end or a feeling that is difficult to put into words. Purpose can be shared, or it can be unique.

Purpose changes over the life span. For many of you, having children gave you a sense of purpose. Recognizing that you were responsible for someone other than yourself and that you were in charge of their care and safety was a powerful and potent motivator.

Or maybe you felt a calling and, either by a direct route or by circumnavigating your universe, you came to understand that there is intention, direction, and meaning not just in what you do but also who you are in doing it.

Discovering Your Purpose

Discovering who you are meant to be isn't always fun. Often people discover purpose and meaning because of negative experiences. Maybe you have had to work through dark legacies of trauma arising within your family or occurring in the environment you grew up in. This may have resulted in your having a sense of purpose to never repeat such things again.

These experiences are supported by our cultural beliefs, especially in our younger years. Because there is no clear demarcation between "doing" and "being," our industrialized, Western Judeo-Christian culture puts more emphasis on the doing. When your "doing years" are done, you may find yourself on the sidelines wondering what is it that you are supposed to do now.

So Now What?

Much of what I do in therapy is about uncovering beliefs that have gone unchallenged for a lifetime. Here are some that might resonate with you:

1. "Now that I'm retired, I have nothing to do."
2. "My kids are grown. They don't need me anymore."
3. "When I was working, I had a reason to get up in the morning."
4. "My mind doesn't work the way it used to. I'm afraid I am losing it."

These beliefs are rooted in our Puritan work ethic. While that ethic has a lot going for it, it is primarily skewed toward the "doing" aspect of purpose. Uncovering the "being" elements of our beliefs can be very rewarding. For example, the statements just listed can be reframed to read:

1. "Now that I'm retired, I need to learn new ways of filling my day."
2. "Now that my kids are grown, I can expand my definition of 'family' to include others who might need me to love and support them."
3. "When I was working, I developed habits that got me going. I need to develop new habits that will motivate me now."
4. "I notice that I pay attention to different things now, and sometimes I find myself daydreaming and not focused at all."

Ways of Finding Purpose as We Age

We can find purpose and meaning in quieter ways as we age. Wonderful ways to connect include meditation, yoga, or participation in a group spiritual practice drawing on traditions thousands of years old. In coming together to learn and share spiritual teachings, you may experience clarity and feelings of belonging to something greater than just yourself. In practicing alone, you may feel connected in a wholly different way to your mind, body, and spirit.

Or maybe you identify with a cause, and your commitment to doing something for others gives you a sense of purpose. Working together with others reinforces our value as an individual and builds skills not just in achieving results but also in collaborating.

You may find yourself pursuing creative avenues such as painting, writing, dance, or music. These areas of self-expression often result in finding purpose and meaning in the *process* of creating. The focus here is on exploring rather than discovering. It is not about what you create, but about what you learn about yourself in the process of creating.

Purpose Has Energy

Purpose is very much like a stream of water making its way to the ocean. It may start small and encounter all kinds of obstacles, yet it persists and, when joined by other streams, turns into a creek, then becomes a mighty river, and finally empties into the ocean.

When your sense of purpose "dries up" or becomes "dammed," you chafe because there is no direction, no action. When you have to work around barriers, you get creative and find ways that may seem to take you backward or in a wide arc. Inevitably this process takes you closer to your goal or end point. When others partner with you because they share the same sense of purpose or at least are in harmony with what you are doing, the energy is magnified and the burden lessened.

Purpose Is Kinetic

When purpose runs unobstructed, it can seem overwhelming. You may shrink from the responsibility and discipline purpose demands of you. On the other hand, when it fades or no longer excites you, you may think of starting over somewhere else, quitting, or even giving up altogether.

Your purpose in life may not be evident to you. You may feel that you have lost all sense of meaning and have nothing left to live for. Or you may just be finding the courage to throw off the bonds of externally imposed expectations and beginning to seek out what makes you feel alive. Give yourself permission to "know what you know," and then—gently, persistently, and with humility—let your purpose reveal itself.

GIVING AND RECEIVING

Originally published September 23, 2018

FINDING MEANING AND PURPOSE IN your life is essential, especially when you are reflecting on your past and facing your mortality. One strategy to find meaning is to be of service to others. Being of service and giving back can take many forms, including volunteering your time, donating money, and mentoring and sharing your expertise. There is plenty of need in this world, and there is enormous benefit in giving. As one self-help guru said, "Givers gain!"

Volunteers make up a powerful workforce across this nation. In many communities they are the backbone of social services for all age groups. Whether volunteering takes the form of delivering Meals on Wheels, providing rides to medical appointments, or visiting skilled nursing facilities with pets or programs, these activities seem to address our very human need to be of service. And there is no question that the satisfaction that comes from giving is immeasurable.

Giving is An Act of Generosity

Giving is an act of generosity. You may be especially prone to using this strategy if you grew up being told, "It is better to give than receive." Many of us consciously or unconsciously use it as a strategy to cover up feelings of insecurity or to make sure that others are beholden to us.

When I am in the position of being a giver, I have the added benefit of social approval and the reassurance that I am OK. I also am in control. Being a giver can be a way to manage and control situations.

On the other hand, there is a downside to being a giver all the time. If you are forever giving, you may not have much experience receiving. Inevitably, as a person ages, the balance tips; once the giver, you now become the receiver. It is essential for us to find a balance between giving and receiving so that we can experience the love, assistance, and the care we need as we age.

Receiving

Receiving can be quite difficult, as it suggests that somehow you are no longer competent, in charge, or able to do things on your own. This can bring up feelings of helplessness and vulnerability. After all, receiving is an act of trust. As we age, we will need to practice receiving lots of different kinds of help from others. Many of us will end up needing some kind of caregiving. We may need someone to take us to doctor's appointments. We may need someone to pick up food or medicine. We may need someone to help us with our most intimate and personal of functions.

These needs may be met by family members or strangers. Ours is a generation that will be relying on the kindness of strangers, because so many of us did not have children. As our numbers grow, so will our need for support and care, especially if we are to remain in our homes.

Finding Good Help

Finding trained and reliable caregivers is a challenge that many of you may have already encountered. The challenge is only going to become more intense. When you are at your most vulnerable—say, after surgery—it would be useful to have a set of skills to let others know your needs and limitations as well as your strengths.

A common complaint in my work is that folks who are being cared for in their homes are often treated like infants. Typically, this complaint is directed at care providers (professional and hired) who are more focused on completing their tasks than engaging with their clients or patients.

To be fair, our care system is not designed for engaging. Caregivers may not have the time or curiosity to find out more about you and may feel caught between productivity requirements and the need to get to the next case. Being able to speak up and just say, "Please take a moment to talk with me before you start your procedures!" could be a game changer.

Thank You

Receiving also takes on spiritual meaning. Aging comes with many gifts; some are more welcome than others, but most can be received with gratitude and grace. Receiving blessings from others is a universal way of acknowledging our connectedness and shared vulnerabilities. As Meister Eckhart said, "If the only prayer you ever say in your entire life is thank you, it will be enough."

Practicing receiving is actually an excellent strategy to increase your capacity for staying engaged as you age. Practicing receiving may be as simple as letting others hold a door open for you or carry packages to your car. Receiving may be more challenging when you let your child take on responsibilities like managing finances or hosting a holiday celebration. Practicing receiving may be even more intimidating if you need to have your child bathe you or change dressings. As you read this paragraph, if you find yourself thinking about how these needs would impact your life, you probably have a good indication that you have some planning to do!

Power of Prayer

Receiving can happen in ways you may not even be aware of! Research shows consistent positive benefits when people pray for you. Studies done at Stanford University and across the nation have been replicated with the same outcomes. Being prayed for (or included in the prayers of others) appears to reduce levels of stress, tension, anxiety, and feelings of hopelessness. In many instances, people who were prayed for in these studies enjoyed several extra months of life and were able to die peacefully, feeling loved and cared for.

Former president Jimmy Carter and his wife, Rosalynn Carter, offer an inspiring example of the benefits of giving and receiving over the life span. As people of faith, President and Mrs. Carter continue to remain engaged in their local church, where they teach Bible study. Both are active in Habitat for Humanity, and the president, along with other world leaders, is actively pursuing peace and tolerance through the foundation, The Elders. Both the President and Mrs. Carter eat well, exercise, and continue to challenge their minds, bodies, and souls.

Using these strategies will help you to stay engaged across the life span and will act as a profound antidote to loneliness and isolation. Practicing receiving as well as giving will bring balance to your life and open up possibilities that you had no idea existed.

GRATITUDE

Originally published October 21, 2018

I WAS SCHEDULED TO BE at a friend's house one evening not long ago. We had made a date to watch the Pixar film *Coco*. The DVD I had ordered online was delayed several times, making me grouchy; when it finally arrived, I wasn't sure whether I was up for watching it. It was the end of a long day that was filled with ups and downs (literally) and much travel, all of which had left me tired and achy. I felt as if the world was just giving me a bunch of extra stuff to deal with. I texted my friend to see if she was still up for watching the movie. And she texted back: "Yes!"

Truth be told, I would have been just as happy to put on my jammies, curl up in bed with some hot cocoa, and forget about the world for the moment. The ceaseless coverage of politics; the outrage (faux and real) over the murder of a reporter; and ongoing suffering for the folks in Florida, Texas, Syria, and Indonesia were all taking a toll on me. I'm not sure I have the bandwidth for the suffering that seems to be offered up on a daily basis. And, for some neurotic reason unfathomable to me, I feel guilty for not being able to do better.

But, instead, I got in my car, picked up some dinner for the two of us, and went over to my friend's house. I am so glad I did! We ate together, shared our day, celebrated our friendship, and watched the movie. I came home tired but restored. I had a good cry (it is a *great* movie) and that is usually a release for me. I got into bed and fell into a deep sleep.

The next morning, I got up at my usual time, warmed up a cup of coffee, got on my stationary bike, and exercised. I watched the news, checked my email, read the headlines, and took a long hot shower. And it stuck me just how incredibly blessed I am.

Blessings

I live in one of the most beautiful parts of the world. I work with people who are heart-centered and caring—who rise each day to help and support other human beings unable to care for themselves. I have access to fresh food and comfortable shelter, and long hot showers. I have choice in where I go, whom I meet with, or whether I interact at all.

I have freedom to worship, freedom to write, and an audience who read what I write and give me feedback.

I can get in my car and drive to the ocean, or I can sit at my desk and talk to and see colleagues who live halfway around the world. When I am "bored," I can put down my book, pick up a remote, and turn on a TV show or movie, or I can listen to one of the great orchestras of the world play Beethoven.

I have access 24/7 to the wisdom of philosophers, poets, artists, and academics who have thought and written about the human condition, life and death. I have at my fingertips inspirational videos, audio recordings, and essays that help to make sense of this incredibly difficult and painful era we are living in. I can study with living masters who are teaching courses on death and dying. And I can share a great movie with a dear friend.

Día de los Muertos— Day of the Dead

If you haven't seen *Coco*, it is all about the Mexican celebration, Día de los Muertos— Day of the Dead. The theme is about remembering. But the movie is about so much more. It is also about following a dream, of being willing to go against tradition and speak up for essential truths. It is about believing in something greater than self. It is about loss and love, and what it means to be human. It is about transitions and the undeniable fact that love seems to transcend time and memory.

The tradition calls for an altar that includes pictures of deceased loved ones; there, people place offerings (*ofrenda*) of foods these loved ones enjoyed and drinks to quench their thirst. At this time of year, the veil between the world of the dead and living is thin, and it is easier for both to trespass, even for just a brief time, into each other's domains. The tradition draws on Mesoamerican roots incorporating the Catholic calendar (All Saints' Day), the maize harvest, the blooming of marigolds, and the monarch butterfly migration.

Memory of Loved Ones

But at its core, this celebration is the expression of gratitude: The commitment of the living to care for the memory of those who have died. Of keeping alive the hopes and passions that have been passed down—as well as the promise of reunion, as we all inevitably will make the transition.

I am presently taking a class on dying with a living master in the Tibetan Buddhist tradition. Like Día de los Muertos, this tradition has rituals for making offerings and bringing gifts for the gods. It also invites a gratitude practice as a way of letting go of attachments to this form and freeing the body so the "soul" can move into the next experience. In this Tibetan tradition, preparation for dying is considered as valuable as preparation for living. The core teaching is that dying is just part of a continuum that exists subtly all around us, demonstrating how foolish we are to resist or fear it—ashes to ashes; dust to dust.

Gratitude

I have the privilege of conversing with many of my patients about death. I often initiate these conversations, but patients gratefully enter into them, with comments such as "I can't talk to others about this, but it is always on my mind." Without fail, the conversation quickly becomes one about gratitude—occasionally regret, but most frequently appreciation and thankfulness for all that has become the narrative of that person's life.

I invite you to find ways to express gratitude. I invite you to find ways to converse with others about death and life and what your hopes, fears, and expectations are. I invite you to celebrate, in whatever your preferred tradition, the remarkable opportunity we are given to be feeling beings. And, by all means, do see *Coco!*

THREE LOSSES

Originally published February 24, 2019

> *Trigger*
>
> Gaze at the photo, into the calm face
> next to yours, sunlit moment suspended
> in strange substance of time. Forget for a moment.
> Then remember.
> Shock floods in, film unspools, zipping
> down in snaky rings on the floor, never
> to be recoiled; accident replays in your mind,
> smoky wreckage spills at your feet. Nothing
> to be done. Weep, curse, step out. Move on.
>
> –Carol Mikoda

LOSS IS AN INEVITABLE EXPERIENCE that has to be faced as we grow older. It is usually unwelcome, is sometimes unexpected, and frequently demands that we make changes we would prefer not to make. There are many kinds of losses, each with a different trajectory and each with different consequences. Basically, though, there are three types of losses: loss of place, loss of person, and loss of purpose.

Loss of Place

Loss of place and the consequences of moving have different impacts as we age. For example, elders often experience grief and disconnection when adult children move away, especially if there are grandchildren. There can also be regret and shame, especially if the move turns out not to be what was hoped for or expected.

Similarly, there can be an experience of grief and disorientation when elders leave the place where they spent their working lives and move into a retirement community, an independent living community, or long-term care. These stressful and often emotional experiences are intensified if there is little or no choice involved.

Loss of "place" also occurs with changes in status. Going from "working" to "retired" is an example of such a change. My husband went through a profound period of grief after he retired. He had loved his work and all that went with it. His change in status from working to retired left him feeling that he no longer mattered. He addressed his grief by re-creating himself and finding work that challenged his mind while staying aligned with his values.

Loss of Person

I don't know that there is any way to prepare for loss of a loved one (including a pet!). It is something we all will experience. Loss of person can happen at any age. As more and more of us are living longer, though, this loss may not be experienced until we are much older.

Boomers were the first generation to achieve the goal of keeping death truly at arm's length for a remarkably long period of time. Previous generations had to contend with polio, smallpox, and flu. Infection and pneumonia killed people and shortened the life span. With the discovery of penicillin and vaccines for polio, mumps, measles, chicken pox, and smallpox, we are better able to keep death at bay. We can now reasonably expect to live well into our sixties and seventies.

Boomers are also the first generation to experience loss of person *without* death. This is the scourge of Alzheimer's disease. Although dementia has been around for many generations, the total number of boomers with dementia surpasses anything in prior generations *because* so many of us are living longer. The loss of "person" here is not about physical life and death, but the loss of formerly shared memory and history that are now accessible only by the one without the disease.

Loss of Purpose

Then there is loss of purpose. This has no time constraints but does happen more frequently to those of us who are aging. Loss of purpose can leave you feeling useless, hopeless, and invisible. It takes a physical and emotional toll. Let's face it. We are prized for our abilities to *do*. When we no longer are producing, we become less valuable.

Purpose gives meaning to both the task and the individual doing the task. In cultures that value people for who they are, and not just what they do, we see less despair among the aging. Finding purpose in life after working may be challenging for some. For others, this "second bloom" provides depth and meaning that far exceeds attainments from earlier years.

Giving Voice to Loss

After my husband died, I found great solace in reading poetry and listening to music. While it was beneficial and essential for me to attend a grief support group to share and work through my deep sense of loss, what was most healing and ultimately carried me through the years of grieving was the work of artists: Musicians who wrote haunting music in a minor key. Poets whose words cut through and entered my broken heart and soul like a laser. Artists whose compositions captured the moments of isolation, despair, pain, and desolation arising out of loss.

Somehow these evocative, heart-centered pathways cut through the nagging, incessant inner voice that said I would never find wholeness again. These artworks let me know I was not alone in my loss. They offered a pathway to connect to my pain and, through that connection, reconnect with the world. And that was enough. Artists, in their expression of their art, connected with me and helped me connect with my feelings. That process is what helped heal me and the disconnection that arises from loss.

Some Additional Thoughts

Grief and depression may share some qualities, but they are very different in terms of how to best address the symptoms and support the person who is experiencing distress because of a loss. Offering support is often difficult for friends and caring others who find their own distress triggered by the intensity of reaction by the person who is grieving or depressed. What is most beneficial for both depression and grief is empathy. This means listening and not trying to fix or distract the person from his or her feelings.

BECAUSE I COULD NOT STOP FOR DEATH . . .

Originally published June 23, 2019

MY LOCAL COMMUNITY THEATER RECENTLY produced *The Belle of Amherst*. The actress playing Emily Dickinson brilliantly captured the wistfulness of the poet as I had always imagined her from looking at daguerreotypes of her. Emily reads this poem in the second act of the play:

> *Because I could not stop for Death —*
> *He kindly stopped for me —*
> *The Carriage held but just Ourselves —*
> *And Immortality.*
> *We slowly drove — He knew no haste*
> *And I had put away*
> *My labor and my leisure too,*
> *For His Civility —*
> *We passed the School, where Children strove*

At Recess — in the Ring —
We passed the Fields of Gazing Grain —
We passed the Setting Sun —
Or rather — He passed Us —
The Dews drew quivering and Chill —
For only Gossamer, my Gown —
My Tippet — only Tulle —
We paused before a House that seemed
A Swelling of the Ground —
The Roof was scarcely visible —
The Cornice — in the Ground —
Since then — 'tis Centuries — and yet
Feels shorter than the Day
I first surmised the Horses' Heads
Were toward Eternity —

This week, Death kindly stopped for a colleague of mine and for a former patient. Both these people had lived good lives, filled with purpose and meaning, and replete with love and joy. In their last days they had also struggled with shuffling off their mortal coil. In stopping for them, Death ended what those of us who knew them considered suffering.

Keeping Death Waiting

One of the nascent truths of aging in the twenty-first century is that Death is waiting longer and longer to stop.

VALUING OURSELVES AS WE GROW OLDER

Not all that long ago, average life expectancy was a mere sixty-four or sixty-five years. In my years working with aging adults, I have seen an incredible variability in functioning that cannot be reduced to chronological age. I know people in their eighties who are younger than people in their sixties!

Chronological age is only one measure of "age-ing." Birth is the onset of life, and Death is the terminus. What happens in between needs to be measured by more than just the passage of time! As a culture we seem to place great value on the first part of the arc of life. For whatever reason, we have developed a bias against getting old. Because that bias is focused on youth and staying young, aging has become something to put off, delay, forestall, and deny. As the inevitability of aging and death occupies more of our consciousness, fear and loathing frequently appear.

Ours is not a culture that values old people or embraces death as a natural extension of life. Yes, there are those who are aware about death, and many have written about it (Emily Dickinson, for example), but this awareness is not common. One of the consequences of having so many boomers aging en masse is that we will collectively be forced into reckoning with death.

Denying that we will die just doesn't seem to me to be a useful strategy. Adding years to my life, if that life is filled with physical limitations, pain, or suffering, doesn't make sense as a goal. Sustaining life when there is no hope of recovery seems cruel. I don't have any attribution for this quote, but it brings this topic into perspective: "Nobody gets off this planet alive."

Because of the age group I work with, I get to have lots of conversations about quality of life when fewer years remain. I am so grateful for these conversations. What I have learned is that there are very few places where death can be talked about frankly and openly. Here in the United States, we have, in just a few generations, taken death out of the house and sequestered it in hospitals and nursing homes. Dying in a hospital is a clinical protocol. Dying in a nursing home is less formal but still an experience filled with strangers. One alternative gaining in popularity is hospice.

Hospice

As it has evolved, hospice in the United States today is actually an extension of our medical system. Those who are eligible for Medicare will find services provided by hospice are reimbursed, including pharmaceuticals (for comfort care), medical equipment, and access to care. Hospice offers a compassionate alternative to the "full code" approach of keeping someone alive using all means available.

In order to access these services, you need to be diagnosed with a terminal illness that has shortened your life expectancy to six months or less. Few people, however, access hospice early on. Sadly (at least in my mind), the average hospice stay was only twenty-three days back in 2015. As we approach the end of our shelf life, odds are that more and more of us will be living with chronic, life-limiting illnesses. There are not enough beds in our hospitals and nursing homes to care for us. I can say with some assurance that more hospitals and nursing homes will not be built to accommodate the boomer surge. Given that prospect, it makes practical sense to explore other options.

I cannot stress enough the value of beginning a conversation about what is important to you as age, especially concerning how you want to die. One essential step is completing a "physician orders for life-sustaining treatment" (POLST) form (polst.org/). This will let your family members, friends, emergency personnel, and treatment providers know and understand your wishes.

If you are like Emily Dickinson, you may not be stopping for Death. But Death will, kindly or unexpectedly, someday stop for you.

HAPPY BIRTHDAY, MOM!

Originally published September 15, 2019

MY MOTHER WOULD HAVE TURNED one hundred this week. She actually made it to eighty-nine, and for most of those years she was vibrant, engaged, confounding, and challenging (this assessment is from a daughter's perspective). I have now had eleven years to reflect on who my mother was, and with each passing day, I find myself humbled, as life is now handing me similar experiences.

Now that I am dealing with the challenges of arthritis and widowhood, I have much more compassion for what my mother went through. In this and in so many areas, I find myself offering apologies to her for failing to have understood what her challenges really were and not expressing my admiration for how incredibly stalwart she was in facing and overcoming them.

Party Time!

If she were still here, we would be having a blowout of a party. My mother loved a good party. Minimal expectations would be to have a family gathering at the roadside restaurant where the family has gathered for generations. We would start with drinks at the bar, then be seated in the private room. Ordering from the menu, my mother would choose "Poor Man's Lobster," onion soup, the salad bar, and a baked potato. (For a woman who never weighed more than 110, she could put away a meal!) Coffee and dessert would follow, although how she had room for them was beyond me!

She would systematically work her way through all the food and all the while be engaged in conversation, reminiscences, and storytelling. As she aged, these stories took on that oft-repeated tempo. Listeners would wait patiently, already knowing the story's arc, but too polite to interrupt. We would laugh in the appropriate places and appear to be surprised at the endings. I suspect my mother was aware of just how patronizing this was, but she was too much the doyenne to call us out on it.

VALUING OURSELVES AS WE GROW OLDER

Dying at Home

My mother's greatest fear was that she would have to leave the family home and go into assisted living. The family home had seen generations be born and die in it. It was a bit museum-like, filled with furniture, books, artwork, and knickknacks that triggered memories and provided comfort. The home also was a beast to care for and presented challenges including only having one bathroom on the upper floor and needing modernization in the kitchen and basement. If it had been economically feasible, having a staff such as Downton Abbey had would have made my mother's life much less taxing.

My husband and I did our best to keep my mother in that home as long as possible. We paid for remodeling and landscaping. We made sure appliances were up to date and in working order. But age and infirmity finally caught up with my mother and the house. She was unable to climb the stairs to her bedroom, and she began to fall more frequently. Her safety needs trumped her emotional ties to the house. On an August afternoon, I transferred my mother from the family home to a lovely assisted living facility across town. It was the hardest thing I have ever done.

Forced to Move

My mother went into a numbed state for almost two years. While she understood at some level that she could no longer manage in her home, her heart was broken in leaving it. The place she moved to was filled with loving, caring people, but they were not family, and their very presence was a daily reminder her of inability to stay independent. I, on the other hand, found myself actually sleeping better, no longer having to worry that my mother was lying on the floor, helpless.

Time healed some of these feelings. My mother's personality eventually emerged from her grief, and she demonstrated a quality she had had all her life—the ability to draw others to her and make them feel special. Her caregivers delighted in her stories and went out of their way to see that she was loved and cared for. She would call me on Sundays and tell me the latest gossip and share with me the new friends she had made. These calls went a long way in helping me to manage my guilt and feelings of having failed my mother.

The Final Gift

Eventually, my mother succumbed to a combination of cognitive and physical decline. She was transferred to long-term care, where she stayed for several months. I received a call from the nursing staff that my mother's life was nearing its end. I was able to be with her, arriving just hours before she died. Truly, this was her final gift. I shared the news with my cousins and family friends.

Here is what I wrote:

> *Hello All—Mom died peacefully tonight at around 10:00 pm. She was resting comfortably, listening to Yo Yo Ma play Mozart. She had wanted her body donated to science; however, she had lost so much weight that it wasn't viable. Instead she will be cremated. She did not suffer, and was cared for by wonderful people—to the end, my mother had a way of charming everyone she came in contact with—such a sweet soul.*
>
> *I find myself in many ways relieved that she is no longer physically in pain—her kyphosis (hunchback) and arthritis were quite taxing, and her heart condition made it difficult for her to sustain activities. I also find myself relieved that she no longer is experiencing anxiety.*
>
> *With that said, I am adrift without my anchor to family. She was the one who remembered the birthdays, recorded the special events, and kept in touch—*

Reflecting and Celebrating

This week, as my mother's hundredth birthday comes around, I find myself celebrating who she was. I have revised so many of my thoughts and feelings—a gift that age has brought me. Her gifts of how she lived her life continue to inform who I am and how I want to age. Most of all, I am learning to forgive myself. Happy birthday, Nonnie!

WAITING

Originally published October 20, 2019

This Moment

Whatever we may think about this moment, our practice is just to return to it. This moment is where all beings exist. Even though we have doubts and fears, even though we ask, "Why do I have to die?" no answer appears. Only this moment is Real. There's no escaping this moment. All beings—including doubt and fear—drop off in this moment.

–Dainin Katagiri, *You Have to Say Something; Manifesting Zen Insight*

I AM VERY GOOD AT waiting. I have developed a full skill set in this art form. For me, waiting started when I was a baby. I am adopted, so I had to wait for a family. From the very beginning I learned to wait. Mind you, I don't actually have any real memory of waiting for a family—just stories told to me over and over—but I have constructed a Hollywood-worthy narrative about waiting to be adopted

I mention this waiting thing because it seems that I am doing a lot of waiting right now. I'm waiting for clothes to dry. I am waiting for goods to be delivered. I'm waiting for hip surgery. I'm waiting to catch a bus to the airport. I'm waiting for food to cook. I'm waiting for money to be deposited. I'm waiting for seasons to change. I'm waiting for my headache to go away. I'm waiting for test results. I'm waiting for daylight savings time to end. I'm waiting for my book to be published. I'm waiting to become famous. I'm waiting to fall in love again. I'm waiting to feel safe. I'm waiting for Trump to be impeached. I'm waiting for traffic to get moving again. I'm waiting for things to return to normal. I'm waiting to die.

Types of Waiting

Seems to me I am spending a *lot* of time waiting. I have learned a thing or two about how I wait. There is my anxious waiting. This kind of waiting is in anticipation of something. I become short-tempered when deliveries are delayed. I become anxious when test results aren't immediately available. I experience distress when I am needing to be somewhere at a specific time and I have to rely on someone else to get me to the appointment. These experiences of waiting are incredibly unsettling because I have little or no control over the actual delivery system and the people providing the service. All I can do is wait.

Of course there is happy anticipation, too. Waiting for the birth of a grandchild; waiting for a birthday or anniversary; waiting for a massage; waiting for a movie, concert, or play to start; waiting for food to come out of the oven. These experiences of waiting are stimulating, even though I have to accept that I have no control over the delivery systems or people involved.

Bus Terminal Waiting

In the 1960s and 1970s, I spent a lot of time waiting in Greyhound bus stations. I was dependent on this mode of transport because I didn't own a car, I couldn't afford the train ticket or airfare, and the bus routes actually served the smaller communities I needed to get to. Greyhound bus terminals were places where I honed some of my waiting skills. I learned how to observe without being intrusive. I learned how to feign sleep and still send out vibes of "don't tread on me!" (I had been cautioned that bad people could be found in Greyhound bus terminals.)

On one trip across country, I ran low on funds and had to panhandle in order to get change to make a phone call and have someone pick me up at the bus station. That experience was eye-opening!

In those days, Greyhound bus stations ranged from the brightly lit terminal in downtown Chicago, active 24 hours a day, to quiet, roadside gas stations where the "stationmaster" was the store owner, who not only sold tickets to passengers but also loaded the bull sperm that was being delivered from farmers to breeders.

Announcements in the larger terminals came over the public address systems, with prerecorded voices identifying well-known and lesser-known stops. "Greyhound service to Milwaukee with stops in Kenosha and Racine . . ." fought for precedence over "Now arriving from St. Louis . . ." or "Now departing for Cincinnati . . ." The sounds of the air brakes and smells of idling diesel engines are still prominent in my memory banks.

Airport Waiting

It has been eons since I have traveled on a Greyhound bus. Nowadays, I hone my waiting skills in airports. It is a different experience, although there are some similarities. Boarding strategies are still required, and I have adapted mine to fit the ritualized queuing before getting on a plane. Exchanges of pleasantries seem fewer and offerings of kindness seem less frequent in airports when compared with my memories of these interactions in bus stations. In truth, this impression may be more reflective of who I am now and who I was then.

Instead of occupying my wait time with movie magazines and paperback novels, nowadays I distract myself with my Kindle or my cell phone. Occasionally I people-watch, but truth be told, I don't find that many interesting characters to observe. Engaging a stranger in conversation seems very intrusive, especially since so many of them have their eyes glued to their screens. So my strategies for managing my waiting have changed, but not the waiting itself.

A Different Kind of Waiting

At this stage of my life, the things I am waiting for carry deeper meaning. Now I am systematically looking for inner quiet. Now I am seeking a balance between my desires and my needs. Now I engage with thoughts of what will happen when I die and what I want to leave behind as my legacy.

Waiting is no longer something to be endured. It is an opportunity for me to explore where my "now" actually intersects with my "becoming" and with my "was." These are subtle markers, and I frequently find myself slipping out of "now" into "next" or "past." That is why the quote that begins this blog spoke to me.

In Death's Waiting Room

I use my Greyhound bus station waiting room metaphor with many of my patients when we discuss waiting, especially if that waiting involves contemplation of death. We seem to share similar memories of spending time in such places. It personalizes the experience and somehow takes some of the unknown out of the equation.

All that will happen is that we will board the bus. The friendly driver will take our baggage and store it under the carriage, take our ticket, and then close the door with that hydraulic "whoosh." The air brakes will be released, the gears will be engaged, and we will leave the station for the final time.

GENERATION GAPS

Originally published November 3, 2019

I READ A STORY IN the *New York Times* this week about millennials and Gen-Zers and their frustration with us boomers (). Three things struck me in reading this piece. First was the cyclical nature of the generation gap, which boomers experienced when rock and roll ruined our morals and the Beatles, with their long locks, blew the socks off our parents. Second was how the focus has shifted to millennials calling out boomers who have failed to address and take responsibility for the current state of our environment. Finally, and perhaps most perversely, the entire article was written from the point of view of millennials who are calling out boomers by selling products (so-called "meme-to-merch") on social media.

Meme as Marketing

Taking each of these aspects one by one, let's look at the marketing campaign first. Gen-Zers are taking the phrase

"OK, Boomer"; putting it on clothes, artwork, and other surfaces; then selling these products online. The campaign is capitalist and entrepreneurial in spirit, artistic in execution, and ironic and funny in its castigation of us old farts who don't care enough about the world to save it. "OK, Boomer" is now a meme-to-merch social media sales pitch. It is dismissive and denigrating; as Lorenz writes, "monetizing the boomer backlash is their [Gen-Zers'] own little form of protest against a system they feel is rigged." The meme is, however, derivative.

As with most memes, there is a modicum of truth in what is being held up for scorn. I frequently wonder what has happened to our generation. We had such aspirations: peace, equality, justice, access to quality weed and good music.

Lost Our Way

Where did we lose our way? Was it because peace wasn't achievable just by marching in protest? Was it because equality is a concept that has many permutations and frequently is put on the back burner once I have my share of the pie? Was it because justice is a living thing that needs more than blind adherence to rules and regulations and requires each of us to take responsibility for our actions and their effect on others? Was it because good weed was way too easy to get and smoking it felt better than dealing with the pain and suffering it numbed us to? When was that day when the music died?

How did our generation elect the current Congress? We had Kennedy! How did we let our government become so corrupt? We got rid of Nixon! When did we become Beaver's parents? We have to face facts. We have not honored the inheritance we received. We have partied too long. It is time we put away those things that numb us and begin to feel the fear and pain and suffering that surrounds us. We are not immune! And we contributed to this state of things.

Generation Gap 2.0

At some level I find comfort in realizing that this is not the first time there has been a generation gap. Although it is not possible to confirm the historical accuracy of the following attribution, I share its sentiment. According to Plato, Socrates once remarked, "The children now love luxury; they have bad manners, contempt for authority; they show disrespect for elders and love chatter in place of exercise. Children are now tyrants, not the servants of their households. They no longer rise when elders enter the room. They contradict their parents, chatter before company, gobble up dainties at the table, cross their legs, and tyrannize their teachers."

OK, Gen-Zers and millennials! What are we going to do about all this? Here is my proposal. It is steeped in Christian values, but if one takes a moment to check around, these values are found in every spiritual practice and culture that has inhabited this planet.

Here are words that inspire me to act.
1 Corinthians 13 New International Version (NIV)

> 1 If I speak in the tongues of men or of angels, but do not have love, I am only a resounding gong or a clanging cymbal. 2 If I have the gift of prophecy and can fathom all mysteries and all knowledge, and if I have a faith that can move mountains, but do not have love, I am nothing. 3 If I give all I possess to the poor and give over my body to hardship that I may boast, but do not have love, I gain nothing.
>
> 4 Love is patient, love is kind. It does not envy, it does not boast, it is not proud. 5 It does not dishonor others, it is not self-seeking, it is not easily angered, it keeps no record of wrongs. 6 Love does not delight in evil but rejoices with the truth. 7 It always protects, always trusts, always hopes, always perseveres.
>
> 8 Love never fails. But where there are prophecies, they will cease; where there are tongues, they will be stilled; where

VALUING OURSELVES AS WE GROW OLDER

there is knowledge, it will pass away. 9 For we know in part and we prophesy in part, 10 but when completeness comes, what is in part disappears. 11 When I was a child, I talked like a child, I thought like a child, I reasoned like a child. When I became a man, I put the ways of childhood behind me. 12 For now we see only a reflection as in a mirror; then we shall see face to face. Now I know in part; then I shall know fully, even as I am fully known.

13 And now these three remain: faith, hope and love. But the greatest of these is love.

Paul askes a lot of us here but offers us a remarkable return on our investment. It is time for us to put away the ways of childhood. We must all grow up and accept responsibility for what resources we consume on this planet. We must take an active stand against injustice and do it not from a place of judgment, but from a far more humble place of acknowledging that we are only acting out of fear of our own shortcomings. I must share all that I know so that others can unburden themselves and we can experience learning from each other instead of competing against each other.

I have faith that we will find a way through what feels like very dark times. I have hope that I will not have to walk that path alone. I can act from love because I have been loved.

LEFT BEHIND

Originally published January 26, 2020

GEORGE BURNS USED TO JOKE, "The first thing I do each morning is to read the obituaries in the newspaper. If I don't see my name, I go make breakfast." Seems as if a lot of people that I know are showing up in the obituaries: Ram Dass, Ravi Shankar, Terry Jones, and Jim Lehrer, to name some famous people, and mothers, sisters, fathers, and brothers of friends, to name people who will be remembered by their loved ones but are unknown outside of those relationships.

Each death brings with it a passel of memories associated with the individual who died and the times shared—whether the person is family or a celebrity. Many of these deaths create a bookmark in my timeline that, when I return to that place, evokes awareness at how truly brief life is, how precious the moments are when shared fully, and how difficult it is for me to be the one left behind.

Last of a Kind

As a youngster I remember reading the story of Ishi, the last of his tribe who survived after the Three Knolls Massacre. There is much about Ishi's life that demonstrates resilience and adaptability, but what haunted me was how alone he must have felt. What I know now is that this was my imagining, perhaps an early expression of compassion. I actually have no idea what his true experience was as the last of his kind, but his story touched something deeply in me.

I had a similar poignant and sorrowful response on imagining what the experience was like for a rare bird, also the last of its kind, crying out for its mate. This is a genetically determined behavior in the bird. I don't know whether the bird had an emotional response or just moved on. I know, for myself, waiting and being met only with silence is anxiety-provoking and very distressful. Today, in our age of instant call-and-response, our capacity for waiting has become almost nonexistent. I can make a strong case that the simmering generalized anxiety that now permeates our world is made worse by this lack of a capacity to wait.

Separation Anxiety in Old Age

The psychological experience of separation anxiety is well researched. We understand at both the biological and physiological levels how the physical body experiences and adapts to separation and loss. Increased levels of neurotransmitters are released in an effort to manage the fight-or-flight response. These include adrenalin, norepinephrine, and cortisol. Prolonged exposure to stress results in overproduction of these neurotransmitters and can negatively impact brain development, particularly in infants and toddlers.

What is less well researched, but now observed more frequently, is how this same pattern of response occurs in older adults. Here the type and frequency of separation changes (for example, death of a partner or spouse, loss of a pet), but the end result is impact to brain functioning, typically a temporary decline in cognitive skills and an increase in depression and anxiety.

It is inevitable that we will experience loss with increasing frequency as we age. The impact of these losses varies, but when they cluster, the experience is intensified and may result in physical, emotional, and cognitive problems. Broadly speaking, the expectations around loss and being left behind tend to be unrealistic and in some cases may result in poor outcomes, including choosing to numb out with alcohol or other substances, withdraw, or fall into depression.

Strategies That Help

For many years, I was angry at my father for leaving me behind. It took a bunch of therapy and several workshops to chip away at the protective barrier I had erected around my heart, thinking I was keeping it safe from being hurt ever again. That strategy didn't keep death away, and others whom I have loved deeply have subsequently left me behind. What I have learned is that the heart does heal. Kindness, self-compassion, patience, and time all play roles in how the healing begins and how long it takes.

What seems to be most helpful, at least according to hospice workers, therapists, and many spiritual traditions, is to allow yourself to fully express and experience the loss. Acceptance of death and loss happens at different times in different states of awareness. For some, thoughts of dying represent release and relief. For others, these thoughts can bring shame and fear. If you are the one left behind, you may experience guilt, anger, or any combination of intense emotions.

According to the folks at the Living/Dying Project, "conscious dying is the process of utilizing the dying process as an opportunity to become more present and loving, an opportunity for profound healing, for spiritual awakening. Eastern traditions such as Hinduism and particularly Buddhism, as well as shamanic traditions, have explicit teachings that guide the dying to a conscious and graceful death."

Keeping Your Heart Open

With each loss I have also learned how to keep my heart open, even though it hurts and I may doubt that the hurt can ever go away. I try to stay aware of my feelings, especially when I am feeling lonely, afraid, or invisible. While I am not always successful in doing so, I get better with practice.

Being left behind is inherently uncomfortable. Learning techniques like meditation, practicing loving-kindness, and finding ways to let go gently and compassionately all help to turn that discomfort into something more soothing. The ache of the loss seems to decrease in intensity not only with time but also with intentional release of tears and revisiting moments of emotions including joy and anger, laughter and intimacy. Extending compassion to self, and being patient with a process that is anything but linear and predictable, are sound techniques to help patch over the gaping wound that loss creates.

FINDING PURPOSE AND MEANING IN A PANDEMIC

Originally published April 19, 2020

I HAVE A LOT MORE time these days to contemplate metaphysical questions. For example, why have I been given a free pass from this pandemic? Others I know are losing loved ones, putting their own lives on the line, and experiencing long-term consequences of treatments designed to save their lives but not ensure they can live those lives the way they did before the pandemic.

I find myself oddly tongue-tied when people share their joy and delight that I am OK, rushing to assure them that although I have gotten through the pandemic in good health, others have not. I look out my kitchen window at neighbors walking what we call the "doggy path" without masks. I silently judge them and wonder why they feel they are the exception and will not get the virus or spread it if they already have it.

Peace or Panic?

These self-observations lead me down many different neurological pathways. I can easily panic when I contemplate the realities of living alone in a pandemic as an older woman. I calm myself by doing familiar rituals like cleaning, laundry, making a meal, having my morning coffee, and acting as if things are as they always have been.

If I allow my imagination free rein, I can leap into a future that entails a lockdown for years and requires others to decide my movements and my fate—a future when my value as a person is weighed against my ability (or lack thereof) to procreate and my drain on society as I continue to consume but not contribute.

The Past Informs the Present

This dystopian future is reinforced by having grown up in the shadow of the atomic bomb and the polio epidemic, as well as having had measles, chicken pox, and the mumps without benefit of any vaccine.

I no longer trust our federal government; I am revisiting my radical beliefs acquired during the Viet Nam War and wondering whether trusting anyone over thirty is ever a good idea. The folly of all these thoughts is crystal clear. Yet they leave their imprints in my mind, like snail tracks.

I find myself making different meanings of this pandemic on a daily basis. It offers me a mirror of my petty thoughts, my unconscious actions, and my ability to adapt and accommodate new challenges. And the pandemic also acts as a projection screen for my prejudices, my fears, and my desire to stay connected to things that are inspiring. These meanings are mixed and conflicting, and the pandemic is providing space for all to coexist.

Renegotiating Reality

The ways in which we interact are needing to be renegotiated because of COVID-19. These negotiations involve physical space and psychological space, as well as redefining intimacy. All aspects of social interaction are open to review. Do we shake hands? Do we bow? Is texting sufficient, or do we need visual contact? Is six feet enough if I am walking? Do I need more space if I am running? How many seats need to be left unoccupied in theaters, arenas, and public transportation systems to ensure I am not spreading or inhaling droplets? How do I read a person whose face is covered? How can I trust someone? What rights do I have if someone unintentionally exposes me to the virus? What responsibilities do I have to ensure I don't expose others? Who decides whose rights are more important?

There will always be those who are unwilling to comply or go along with what is asked of them. And there will always be those who feel they must enforce the rules. Somewhere in the middle are the great masses of us who long for compassionate leadership while forgetting that this is initiated from within. We can turn the tide. We can heal many of our own wounds. We can always find ways to better understand ourselves and each other. And we need each other.

I find myself looking for philosophies that say there is meaning in all that is happening. I come to terms with what seems dire by opening myself to feel the feelings—to look past the immediate, open my emotional and psychological apertures, and see what else is happening.

The New Normal

And here is what I see: the sun is out for a longer period of time each day. New growth is showing up on trees and in the vineyards. Flowers are emerging from the ground and their buds are opening. Folks are reaching out to each other in ways they haven't in a long time. People are changing how they do things, are observing social distancing, are wearing masks, are washing their hands. In spite of vitriol and hyperbole, regular folks are stepping up and checking on their neighbors, shopping for others who can't get to the store, making masks and posting fun videos and jokes online.

There seems to be an irrevocable pull to humanity in most of us. Not all, but most. And for this moment, that is sufficient to give me hope. Now, I have been accused over the years of being a cockeyed optimist, naive, and, frankly, too hopeful. I admit that these are preferred states of mind for me. I can certainly entertain a more dire view of things, and I have been known to make cynical comments, but this isn't my preferred stance, and such thoughts don't provide me with the strength I know I need to survive.

Choice

I am choosing to find purpose and meaning in this pandemic. I am connecting with what I believe is essential to my humanity: understanding the consequences of my actions; accepting responsibility for how I share time, space, and resources; and coming to terms with the inevitability of change that I have no control over and the inevitability of my own death. For today, I am grateful that I am enjoying good health, the love of friends and family, having food to eat and a safe place to sleep. May this be true for all beings, if not today, then someday soon.

Check out the book *Grounded Spirituality* by Jeff Brown.

LET THERE BE LIGHT

Originally published May 31, 2020

Genesis 1 King James Version (KJV)

> 1 In the beginning God created the heaven and the earth.
>
> 2 And the earth was without form, and void; and darkness was upon the face of the deep. And the Spirit of God moved upon the face of the waters.
>
> 3 And God said, Let there be light: and there was light.
>
> 4 And God saw the light, that it was good: and God divided the light from the darkness.

SOMEHOW, WE HAVE LOST GOD and returned to darkness. Somehow, we have given up all that was good and fallen into hell. Somehow, we have chosen to live in darkness, but we need not continue this way.

I was ten years old when President Kennedy was slaughtered in Dallas, Texas, in November 1963. I was in music class. As a nation, we stopped what we were doing and we mourned the man. We felt hope being stolen and the darkness began to descend. As a ten-year-old, I only knew that sadness and grief gripped all the adults around me. And I was sore afraid.

In February 1965, in New York City, Malcolm X was executed. His death was a political assassination of a black leader and was just the beginning. I had a vague awareness of Malcolm X, but I was only twelve, so his death was not immediately impactful in my suburban life.

In April 1968, the Reverend Martin Luther King Jr. was assassinated in Memphis, Tennessee. I was now a much more impressionable fourteen. I had heard Jesse Jackson speak of Dr. King. I had marched with my mother to support civil rights. I had celebrated when my minister went to Washington, D.C., to support Dr. King and join with millions of Americans who were asking for justice for African Americans during the March on Washington.

I remember going out on my back porch and looking up at the heavens as the TV and radio covered the riots that were spontaneously erupting in my hometown of Chicago and in neighboring communities in Detroit, New York, and Los Angeles. I knew the world that I had grown up with had died along with Dr. King.

Just two months later, Robert Kennedy was murdered in Los Angeles. It seemed as if the world was unable to accept any sort of hope or light or promise of equality. I, along with my mother, wept at the needless deaths of individuals who had carried the promise of a brighter, more equitable future for all of us.

Coverage and Context

Television covered all of these moments in history. Walter Cronkite informed the nation of JFK's death. We collectively grieved. We found ourselves following the images of Kennedy's cortege and John-John's salute. Malcolm X's death was covered by mainstream media with a focus on his role in instigating uprisings among Black people (then called Negroes). He was cast as a violent man who called upon Blacks to take up arms against Whites.

Our eyes on the world were filtered through journalists who had reported the evils of Hitler, the rise of communism, and the spread of socialism. We were indoctrinated by pundits and power brokers who brooked no opposition and expected us to fall in line and accept what we were being told for our own good. But the medium of television brought a new and more powerful persuader—pictures in real time of the events as they were unfolding.

Reverend King was sanctified by his followers and vilified by the Federal Bureau of Investigation. Mainstream media coverage of his murder by a southern White man included footage of Reverend King's "I Have a Dream" speech given at the foot of the Lincoln Monument.

Between 1968 and 1970, there was relative calm, except for that nagging conflict on the other side of the world in Vietnam. Protests persisted as casualties were reported; daily more and more young men refused to sign up for the draft or went to Canada. Those who did get drafted were predominantly young men of color who saw service as a means of bettering themselves rather than as valorous service to a nation that disregarded them.

When White students were killed at Kent State University in May 1970, the mainstream media once again covered the events. Disregarded by the media, but no less horrendous, were the killings that same month at Jackson State University, a predominantly Black school.

Nothing Shocks Me

I list all of these moments from my formative years because they have contributed to my inability to be shocked that law enforcement officers kill Black people. These events are no longer outrageous. They have become common. So much so that they don't even make mainstream news.

In the last week, our nation has crossed the threshold of 100,000 deaths due to COVID-19. We have seen the hunting of one Black man by White men and the murder of another in custody of those who were sworn to preserve and protect our communities. These events were shared over and over on social media, on TV, and in newspapers and magazines. Outrage? Just a headline.

Yet we have been here before. As a nation, we have stood on this precipice, not once or twice, but more than five times in our recent history.

Is It Different Now?

What is different this time is that we are all feeling the vulnerability. People of privilege are not immune to COVID-19, although we seem to be numb to the suffering of other fellow beings. COVID-19 has taken more people of color than Whites, giving false witness to a belief that Whites are somehow favored or protected against death and suffering. I am here to bear witness that suffering is not the sole domain of any one skin color. All of us are diminished by every death. Our humanity is stripped when we go about our lives claiming rights that are based on misperception and bad education.

Perhaps it is time to admit that we have stayed in darkness too long. We need to explore our own darkness and surrender to a more potent truth that we need each other. Without finding ways to coexist and collaborate, we will all succumb. When God created this earth, I have to believe, this was not what He had in mind.

NEEDING A LULLABY TO SOOTHE ME

Originally published August 23, 2020

I HAVE NOTICED LOTS OF intense comments showing up in social media posts these days. I am doing my best to take several deep breaths before I respond. In some cases, the posts have been forwarded and later found to contain misleading or just plain wrong information. In other cases, people are stating their positions forcefully, resulting in hurt feelings and blocked connections.

Where I live is very special to me. It has physical beauty, friendly neighbors, good food, and remarkably clement weather. The people here are a lot like me. They think like I do and enjoy the same activities. We have found ways to tolerate our differences, even though those differences are actually not all that significant. Still, since March, I have noticed that I am jumpier. I am quicker to judge and even condemn. I am impatient when things don't go my way. I am so very aware that things have changed. That something that was once very special is missing. I didn't use to be afraid, but now I am.

Erosion of Security

My sense of security has been eroding slowly but steadily since COVID-19 first came on the scene. I wanted to believe that it would be a short-term inconvenience. That was my way of managing the vulnerability I felt. Instead, each day seems to bring more catastrophic mortality and morbidity statistics, delivered by news personalities, elected officials, and persons of varying levels of experience and education masquerading as experts. I have marveled at the numbers of people who never made it through high school biology who have become specialists in epidemiology and who now share their expertise in every venue available.

Information goes a long way in soothing my tender psyche. Unfortunately, I am no longer sure whether the information I have access to is real or not! I have Snopes on speed dial. Yet I am finding, all too often, that the things I want to believe are true, aren't. Giving up my firmly held beliefs is hard because it means that I am that much more exposed and have fewer places to hide.

VALUING OURSELVES AS WE GROW OLDER

Lullabies

When I was a little girl, my mother would sing lullabies to soothe me to sleep. I had a vivid imagination as a child and would frequently find myself sucking my thumb, curled up in a ball, with my stuffed toy to protect me. To this day, I cannot read a Stephen King novel or watch episodes of *The Twilight Zone* because they frighten me to the core—and not in that oddly pleasing way that they frighten so many fans of these genres. No, I would cower beneath the covers and pray that God would protect me.

At some point before I fell asleep, my mother would come in, gently gather me into her lap and reassure me that there was nothing to be afraid of. She had a pleasing soprano that lifted the fear. The rhythm of her rocking along with the predictability of the melody allowed me to relax. In that relaxed state, my mind slowed down, and the terror melted away. I would drift off to sleep and then awaken the next day without the anxiety hangover. Oh, how I miss that experience!

This week, I was awakened by a crack of lightning followed by a sonic boom of thunder, leaving behind a residue of metallic ozone in the air. Normally I love thunderstorms. This time, I was unprepared for the 4:30 am wake-up call from nature! I was *scared*! It felt as if Mother Nature was really angry. It took me a while to soothe myself—actually, more than just a while.

Disconnection

I realized that I am on edge most of the time these days. There is a disconnect between what my rational mind says I am experiencing and what my body-mind says I am going through. I catch myself breathing (a good thing!), but with shallow breaths. I find myself dozing rather than sleeping, and I often wake up feeling tired. Little things provoke huge emotional responses.

I spent time with a group of women whom I greatly admire. We were discussing how we manage change. One said, "I make a plan!" We all agreed that was a good strategy. Then one of the group said, "It only works if you initiate the change. What we are going through now wasn't initiated by any of us. It's like the difference between choosing to leave a job and getting fired. It's almost like we are all being fired from our old lives!"

"You're Fired!"

That sentiment rings true for me. It's as if I have gotten fired from my old life, where I decided what I would do when. Where I chose whether I would go out or stay in.

Where I felt unfettered in hugging people or shaking hands, going to a movie or browsing in a bookstore.

I've only ever been fired from a job once, and the experience has stayed with me all my life. The sense of helplessness. The sense of shame. The realization that I couldn't return to that routine that felt secure ever again. I wondered what would soothe me now.

The answer came to me in one of the lullabies my mother sang to me: "Summertime." DuBose Heyward was the lyricist who penned "Summertime." George Gershwin was the composer who indelibly linked it to melody in *Porgy and Bess*.

> *One of these mornin's, you're gonna rise up singin'*
> *Then you'll spread your wings and you'll take to the sky*
> *But 'til that mornin', there is nothin' can harm you*
> *Yes with Daddy and Mammy standing by.*

TO EVERY THING THERE IS A SEASON

Originally published August 30, 2020

I CONFESS, I AM NOT much of a Bible reader, but I have found words of wisdom within its pages that help me make sense of my world on many occasions. This week the words of Ecclesiastes have been registering. I first remember hearing these words, originally put to music by Pete Seeger, when the Byrds sang "Turn, Turn, Turn." I didn't know then that the words came from Ecclesiastes.

As I have watched our political process unfold over the past few weeks, and experienced the pain and suffering that continues to impact our lives on a daily basis, I was struck by how familiar these experiences would have been to the author of Ecclesiastes, who is believed to have written it around the tenth century BC. ("BC" here means *"before Christ"* not "Before COVID-19.") There are but twelve chapters in this book of the Bible, and each has pearls of wisdom that are helpful reminders to me right now.

What is it about the human experience that we continue to value achievement and acquisition of goods and things over investing in and cultivating kindness and tolerance? The author of Ecclesiastes notes that it is all "vanity and vexation of spirit" and that it will all pass away. He (or she) acknowledges the existence of wickedness and iniquity, oppression and abuse of power, but also explores the effects of wise actions, wise speech, and adherence to the commandments (in this case, ten of them).

Both/And

The reader of Ecclesiastes goes through a rather exhausting experience of considering things "on the one hand . . . and on the other . . ." without coming to a clear conclusion. I suspect the author was a Libra. She (or he) always explores both sides of the question. But what is the question here? What is it that we are needing to find consensus with now?

I am torn between feeling guilty for having all that I have and feeling protective of it. Knowing that things can be lost in a moment from fire or flood or pandemic does little to staunch my desire to acquire more in my attempts to feel safe once again. This desire is more like the addict's attempts to quell the pain of withdrawal by numbing it with the substance that caused the craving in the first place. It is not rational. Only here I am craving safety and security and I am numbing the awareness of my fragility and vulnerability by brandishing an AK-47 and building a wall.

Stop Shouting!

Three sentences jumped out at me in chapters 9 and 10 of Ecclesiastes: "The words of wise men are heard in quiet more than the cry of him that ruleth among fools. Wisdom is better than weapons of war; but one sinner destroyeth much good" (9:16-17).

There is so much shouting going on right now. We can be distracted by those who are making noise, or we can listen to that quiet voice that exists within ourselves. We are all witness to the destruction that has occurred because of what one man, one party, one blind-eyed ruler has tried to do. "Woe unto thee, O land, when thy king is a child" (10:16).

I certainly do not mean to cherry-pick from this book of the Bible. I find fault with those who collect phrases to support their particular point of view, while ignoring those that don't. It is particularly hard to do something like that with Ecclesiastes, because both positive and negative, light and dark, are woven into each chapter. The author asks us to consider both sides and does not suggest there is a preference for one over the other. He (or she) does suggest that there are certain practices that one can follow but does not guarantee any outcome other than this: "Then shall the dust return to the earth as it was: and the spirit shall return unto God who gave it" (11:7).

The final chapter has only fourteen sentences, the last of which encapsulates the folly of expecting one side rather than another to be right: "For God shall bring every work into judgment, with every secret thing, whether it be good, or whether it be evil" (12:14). This sentence gives me some hope for equivalence. It lowers the volume around "my way or the highway" and "I'm right, you're wrong." Still, this sentence leaves me to wait for final judgment—to wait for God to decide. And while I can value the wisdom of these thoughts and words, I am unwilling to wait for Judgment Day to bring this to a conclusion.

A Teaching Story

There is a teaching story about the person walking down a path who suddenly finds herself having fallen in a hole. She frets and fumes, "How did this happen to me? I don't deserve to be in this hole!" But, eventually, she finds a way out and continues on.

Next day, on the same path, the same thing happens. Same conversation. Gets out and goes on her way. Several days (and several falls in the same hole) pass, but now, she is aware of the hole in the path ahead. This time, she still falls into the hole, but her conversation while in there is shorter and she gets out sooner.

Now she is better prepared and, walking down the same path, knowing the hole is ahead, she finds a way around the hole. Having successfully made it to the other side, she celebrates ... and falls backward into the hole.

A few more days pass. By now she has acquired a lot of experience with holes! Finally, after much deliberation, consulting with experts, and making declarations to never make the same mistake again, she walks down a completely different path without holes.

A Different Path?

I have to wonder where we are, as a culture, as a species, as caring individuals, on this path we call life? How many times have we fallen in this hole? It feels so very familiar to me! I want this time to be different. I know that I need to find a different path. One that puts tolerance and love in place of prejudice and fear. It is not a familiar path, but I am tired of falling into the same hole.

PAUSING FOR A MOMENT

Originally published September 27, 2020

> *This post was written just days after the death of Ruth Bader Ginsberg and during a time of great uncertainty regarding the pandemic and our political process. It reflects my own need to connect with something deeper and more predictable.*

THIS MORNING I WOKE IN darkness, aware that somehow, in the past few days, summer had faded away and autumn was taking her place. Then I heard the cry of the geese. Somewhere, deep inside of me, this ancient rhythm of the change of seasons responded to these prompts, and I just paused.

I am a child of the summer. I prefer to wake early and bask in the daylight as it floods the Earth. And I delight in the long, lingering twilight as the sun refuses to quit and give way to the stars at night. I prefer hot days and cool nights, which I found when I moved to Northern California. The energy of summer suits me, inviting me as it does to be productive, playful, and present. Spring has always been a bit elusive, sometimes bursting with energy after a prolonged winter's siege, and other times seeming to last but a day between snow and hundred-degree heat.

But it is autumn that invites reflection for me. The season is an essential pause and a much-needed one. Autumn is like a shepherd who keeps an eye on things from afar but remains vigilant and protective. The crops have come to fullness, and now it is time for their leaves to drop and decay. The winds carry an edge to them, along with a different scent. Without naming it, my inner clock notes the passage of time and begins its own metabolic shift, following some ancient pattern passed down genetically.

Mixed Feelings

I have such mixed feelings about autumn. I love the colors changing. Having grown up in the Midwest and spent time in the East, the majesty of the palette is remarkable. I am old enough to remember the gracious boughs of the Dutch elm before disease decimated these leafy giants. The leaf fall made piles of leaves an engaging plaything, and the smoke from the burning of these piles filled the air with an unforgettable scent of autumn. Then there is the flaunting of color by the maple trees, the true harlots of autumn. Their flamboyant reds, ochres, and scarlet hues cannot be ignored.

Aspen Gold

When I moved west, I was introduced to the extraordinary aspen. Like a coordinated dance line, all aspen trees shift from leafy green to transcendent gold within weeks. Their change in color is initiated by a drop in temperature, and eventually the snow removes what few leaves remain on the branches.

I also fell in love with the Sierra. Yosemite in particular is a sacred spot for me, as it was for John Muir. He knew and loved every inch of the Sierra and shared his love for it in his many writings. He, too, found autumn to be a time of reflection.

> *Climb the mountains and get their good tidings. Nature's peace will flow into you as sunshine flows into trees. The winds will blow their own freshness into you, and the storms their energy, while cares will drop away from you like the leaves of autumn.*

Here in northern California, it is the vines that mark the change in season. Harvest typically occurs in late September, and once the chardonnay and sauvignon grapes are picked, the remaining leaves on the vines turn a muted bronze and gold. The zinfandel, cabernet, and merlot grapes stay on the vine longer, and after the fruit is harvested, these plants' leaves morph into deep purples and scarlets. Since the vines are only three to four feet above the earth, the vista looks like deep shag carpeting against the camel-hair tan of our hills.

A More Powerful Pull

You may wonder why I have chosen to write this post at this time. I have started writing several others, with titles ranging from the "End Times" to "A Call to Arms." There is much to be disturbed about, and there are plenty of causes to support. But it was the geese who reminded me this morning that there is a more powerful pull. These momentary events—sad, frightening, and destabilizing as they are—are distractions from a more profound inevitability.

I mourn the passing of Ruth Bader Ginsberg. I mourn the deaths of nearly one million people around the world from COVID-19. I mourn the loss of trust in government, civility in social discourse, and the predictability in my daily life that I depend on to keep me calm. But, like the geese, I am called to change direction and head home.

This ancient pull of the seasons, the unstoppable shift from harvest to decay, the promise that there will be a summer once winter solstice has occurred, all comfort me in my own moments of doubt. This deeper rhythm, like a strong bass line in a song, will carry me through my temporary fear and sorrow. This is a promise that is kept and has been kept for millennia.

I have a dear friend who is an incredible poet. She, too, sings with the geese. I share her words here because they comfort me, and I hope they will be of comfort to you also.

bud, leaf, jewel, ash

> shimmering symbol of balance and peace
> just one leaf tells all to be told
> bud, leaf, jewel, ash
> no one of us more important than another
> each of us belongs to the other
> bud, leaf, jewel, ash
> each of us has what another one needs
> no hierarch but blended together
> bud, leaf, jewel, ash
> infinity of darkness before finding light
> infinite patience to reach speed
> giving, giving in order to receive
> frigid cold that generates heat
> season always gives way to season
> suffering abounds but change persists
> bud, leaf, jewel, ash

–Carol Mikoda

SANCTUARY

Originally published October 4, 2020

The fires in Northern California are now a yearly occurrence. In 2018, I stayed and watched as the hills around where I live burned. It was four days of smoke, fear, and more fear. While my home did not suffer, friends lost everything. I did not realize the extent to which I carried the trauma of those days.

I RAN AWAY THIS WEEK. Fled. Gave up the ghost. Abandoned my post. It all finally became too much, and so I fled to a place that wasn't in the pathway of raging fires, appeared to have taken appropriate precautions for COVID-19, and held happy memories of better times for me. I have returned home, somewhat chastened, definitely improved in mental state and capacity to face what is a continuing challenge, but also keenly aware of how much I need sanctuary.

I was intimately familiar with the location I chose to flee to. My husband and I had spent untold hours driving around this area, exploring the back roads and dead ends, as well as shopping, dining, and getting to know the locals—even contemplating it as a place where we might retire. It is incredibly beautiful and has a delightful small-town ethos, not just because it actually is a small town but also because it has all the big-city amenities that we had come to expect.

But this time it was different. And different in that slightly off-kilter way, as when the audio is out of sync with the video. The places I remembered were still there, but with different names and with restrictions because of COVID-19. Some of our favorite hidden byways still remained, but they were now filled with new buildings and lacked the quaint, small-town feel. There was an edge to the exchanges with masked store clerks and customer service folks. Lines were long and shelves were thinly stocked.

Unable to Locate

Maybe it was my mood or maybe it was the weather, which was overcast but cool, but I could not find what I longed for: that feeling of relief and letting go that comes from being in a familiar, welcoming place.

I stayed in a perfectly lovely hotel, now barricaded with plexiglass because of COVID-19, but reassuringly hermetically sealed from the room entry to the prophylactic covering on the remote. I felt like a caged animal.

I planned on staying for four days, assuring myself that in that time the danger from fire at home would have decreased and I would have enjoyed a brief vacation. But circumstances conspired to cut the time short. So I returned home.

Not much, if anything, had changed at home. The fires continued to burn, the air continued to be unbreathable, and there were still bills to be paid, calls to be returned, and appointments to be kept. But I had changed. This change is what is so fascinating to me.

Hitting the Reset Button

It was as if I had hit the reset button. I realized that my home is my sanctuary, in no small part because of the miscellaneous items that I unconsciously take for granted. My shower head is adjusted the way I like it. I know just how long it will take for the water to get hot. My coffee setup is organized and the muscle memory to get that brew done requires only that I remember to boil the water. My favorite channels are easily accessed on my TV and radio. My bed has my sheets and my pillows, and my chair is molded to fit my body. The pictures on the walls, always just slightly askew, soothe my soul and bring happy memories to mind.

This level of familiarity is vacated when I am in a new place. The novelty of using a different shower and coffee setup, working a strange TV, and adjusting to unfamiliar pillows and chairs is an effective way to stimulate my aging brain. But when I am depleted emotionally and psychologically, and when I am at my core threatened with extinction, the benefit of that novelty drops to the bottom of the list, and I am left even more fatigued.

I have seen this emptiness in the eyes of people whose homes have been incinerated in the fires. I have seen this surrender in the drooping shoulders of people who have stood in long lines only to be told the forms they need to fill out to start their lives over are located in another line, even longer. I have seen this in the shuffling strides of those who are homeless and now without work or purpose.

Where Can I Be Safe?

Where can I go when home is no longer safe? I am not the first to ask this question. Whether we are women who are physically and economically tied to partners who make life unsafe, or we are among the increasing numbers of people who are becoming climate refugees, where do we go when our homes are no longer a sanctuary?

In reviewing these past few days, I came to the conclusion that I was seeking sanctuary. I was seeking a place of refuge, a place where I would find peace and tranquility. An experience where I would feel connection and belonging. For me, this can be found in nature or in the company of others. What truly brought me "home" was not just returning to my house, but lingering in conversation with friends who reached out to see if I was OK.

To Stay or Go?

I find myself wondering whether my time here in California is spent. I have lived here for forty-one years—the longest I have lived in any one state. While I can go through a checklist of places that present lower environmental risk and are possibly more economically advantageous as I approach retirement, I now realize that what is essential is that I am able to connect with and build community. And that is a daunting prospect in these current times.

I understand better why some people stay behind to protect their property. I have more compassion for those who return and irrationally put themselves in what are unsafe environments. It is hard to leave a place that brings such comfort for the unknown. What all this has taught me is that I am going to have to leave sometime—either by my own choice or because I am forced to leave. The challenge is knowing when to exercise my options.

THE IMPORTANCE OF LEAVING A LEGACY OF VALUES

Originally published February 11, 2018

I WAS READING AN ARTICLE by Vanessa Friedman in the *New York Times* about the fashion designer Carolina Herrera, who, at age seventy-nine, was shifting her focus from creating outfits for the rich and famous (such as Michelle Obama, Renée Zellweger, and Caroline Kennedy) to retiring. That is not a word that Mrs. Herrera sees as fitting for her next new venture, which she called "Global Brand Ambassador." Several things struck me about this article.

First, Mrs. Herrera made it clear that she was not retiring but was "moving forward." I like this attitude. Moving forward is something not often associated with aging! I think this reflects our ageist bias that things slow down as we age, and an unfounded belief that there isn't much to look forward to.

Legacy of Values

Second, the article, while focused on the nuance and intrigue of New York high fashion, underscored an essential principal of aging. It is vital that we intentionally explore and leave a legacy not just of things but also of what is important to us in terms of ideas, values, and principles.

Mrs. Herrera's legacy includes her designs along with her fashion sense, her vision of what a well-dressed woman should look like, and a model of female business leadership in a world dominated by males. Her legacy also includes a skill set of adaptation and accommodation to the demand that something be different each season while retaining a "classic" look that doesn't push potential buyers over the edge.

Generational Transmission of Values and Ideas

Friedman posits that this is "another generational change." This is an interesting phenomenon within families as well as fashion dynasties. When is the right time for the oldsters to hand over the reins?

VALUING OURSELVES AS WE GROW OLDER

What is more and more apparent in our society is that a predetermined age (like Medicare) is merely a benchmark. Mrs. Herrera is only now considering transferring creative responsibility at age seventy-nine. This is a risky business, as Vanessa Friedman notes: "It's a complicated, fraught decision, with its intimations of mortality and loss of control—especially for those whose names are above the door. Some have ignored it (see: Azzedine Alaia who died unexpectedly last November without a succession plan for his business), while others in Mrs. Herrera's peer group have tried to solve it, with varying degrees of success."

Maybe you are not the scion of an international fashion brand focused on ensuring continuation of the name for untold generations to come. Maybe you received special mementos from a beloved grandmother or are finding yourself sharing wisdom previously shared by respected elders. I believe that these are as valuable as Mrs. Herrera's brand. And it pays for you to honor your legacy in the same way.

Curating the Family Valuables

Setting aside time to systematically appreciate and decide what is important to hand down to your children, grandchildren, or other beloveds can be a wonderful shared experience. For example, you can have special storytelling time when you tell your story to other family members or to friends. You can create a "life map," made up of events that are of note in your life, annotated with pictures, drawings, captions, and other creative mixes.

These exercises often get put on the back burner. My husband finally started writing down his memories of childhood summers spent on Lake George in upstate New York when he was in his seventies. These were magical times for him and occurred during historic times for our country. He captured the flavor of the challenges of driving from Connecticut, where his family lived during the rest of the year, packing up the car, and heading into the wilds of the Adirondacks, where roads were sometimes paved and sometimes not, to the easy days of swimming, fishing, and canoeing on beautiful Lake George. While I had the joy of actually staying in the same cabin he spent his summers in when we made a trip back east, my husband's children never did. So the only legacy that remains for them of these times are the brief notes he left behind and my memory of the stories he told.

Collecting Fragments

So often that is all we have of those who have gone before us: Fragments from which we construct a storyline. Wisdom shared. Mrs. Herrera made notes: "The easiest way to look old is to dress young." "Elegance is to be remembered." "Getting old is all the things you have not managed to do." How do you capture your wisdom?

We are living in an age of disposable things. I am saddened about this, since it seems to be undercutting an important value that was passed down to me—namely, that there are things worth preserving. A fine line exists, however, between curating things of value (ideas, mementos, objects) and accumulating things (storing up for some future event or need). I find it ironic that some of the best sellers recently have been books on how to get rid of things!

Exploring the Legacy

One way to manage this tension between letting go and going on is to explore the legacy of the things you received, weigh their value to you in your life, and discuss with others whether they might find these items valuable in their lives. Ideally, we would do so intentionally and with collaboration and cooperation from family, friends, and beloved others.

LEGACY OF PROTEST

Originally published March 25, 2018

This blog was published after thousands of people of all ages gathered across the United States to express a desire for change after the mass shooting at Marjory Stoneman Douglas High School in Florida.

ALMOST FIFTY YEARS AGO, I marched on Washington to take a stand against the war in Vietnam. Passion and commitment to challenging the status quo are a legacy handed down from our founding fathers. Today young people are taking a stand against violence in schools.

Each generation since 1776 has seen its share of hardship born of social, economic, environmental, and political change. During the almost 250 years since the colonists first complained to King George III about the unfairness of the Stamp Act, Americans have been protesting something. This legacy continues today.

The legacy of protest is both dramatic and inspiring. It reflects expressed values of righting wrongs, addressing unfairness and imbalance in society, and raising consciousness while demanding change. Sacrifices made during protests represent both the best and the worst of humanity. Lives have been sacrificed in many movements ranging from civil rights to the environment. That such sacrifice remains necessary is a sad indictment of where we are today as a society.

Shared Legacies

Several legacies are shared with today's protesters. First, coming together, whether in protest or in support of a position, is a way to connect on a deeply personal level. We are, after all, social beings. So much of what we do today is in electronic form. Connecting that way is different neurologically, biologically, and sociologically from what has been our history. Yet, the result appears to be similar. Connection, validation, and a sense of empowerment arise from knowing I am not alone.

Secondly, demonstrating is a powerful expression of participatory democracy. It is not unique to the United States. It is a way for any group to make known a position that is either being ignored or suppressed. Demonstrating for change requires individual leadership, expression of an idea larger than the self, and a call to action.

Thirdly, participants in these events will return to their lives changed by having protested. They will have been changed by the experiences of coming together, participating in something larger than their own individually driven needs, and taking a stand that requires courage. This act of courage is able to be expressed *because* it takes place in a group. Individually expressing dissent is often too risky, and so protests are silently held within.

These experiences, when looked back on, may turn out to be pivotal in the later life choices made by the protesters. Bonds formed by joining in these events may reinforce or, perhaps, change beliefs and values that determine and inform choices made across the life span. These experiences may dramatically change how a life will be lived.

Then and Now

How does this impact us in terms of aging? For many boomers, events such as the Vietnam War, the March on Washington for civil rights, the 1968 Democratic Convention in Chicago, the Moratorium to End the War in Vietnam, and Woodstock marked coming-of-age experiences that highlighted generational and political differences, giving rise to the "generation gap."

For millennials, 9/11, Occupy Wall Street, the Arab Spring, the Women's March on Washington, the #MeToo movement, and the March for Our Lives are seminal events. What will be made of these events as millennials turn 60, 70, 80, and 90 is yet to be determined.

Coverage will include interpretation of speeches made, the strength and weakness of the arguments on both sides, and the likelihood of political change arising from these gatherings. Individually, I suspect people who actively participated will come away feeling charged and inspired. Some may even find themselves transformed by the experience.

Shared Values

Years from now, I hope those who participated, like me, will look back and realize that many of their political beliefs and social values were honed through these assemblies. Coming together in support of things much larger than my daily existence helped me to define my patriotism. Hearing the stories of others who shared my passion but came from different backgrounds opened my heart and mind and helped me become more vigilant about which rights were being undermined or were threatened by demagogues.

I received a legacy from my parents and grandparents in terms of what is required of me as a citizen in this increasingly diverse and aging nation. Specifically, I hold my elected representatives to a higher standard, and when they do not meet that standard, I take steps to see that others are elected in their place. I gained experience in what it means to participate in a representative democracy that requires more of its citizens than just voting. I gained courage in taking a stand with others that allowed me to speak my truth when I was alone or in a small group.

I am inspired by the marchers today. I hope their legacy will include changes to our laws and changes in how we address violence, marginalization, and justice. I know the stories shared by the speakers will touch many lives. I also know the individual experiences arising from coming together for such a powerful cause will resonate across the life span of those who were in attendance.

PASSING THE BATON

Originally published April 8, 2018

I RECENTLY LISTENED TO AN interview with Harry Belafonte, in which he reflected on his friendship with Martin Luther King Jr. Belafonte, who turned ninety-one last month, shared how he had met King at a civil rights protest when they were both in their early twenties. Together, both men made history confronting the inequalities that existed in the South in the 1960s and, along with others, led a movement that profoundly influenced my generation.

1968 saw tremendous conflict across the United States. After King was assassinated in April, riots broke out in Chicago, Detroit, and other major cities. Fear ran deep that Black Americans would seek revenge and White Americans would be their target. Church leaders and civil rights leaders came together, reminding us all that even in our shared grief over the death of Martin Luther King Jr., the work of peaceful protest remained the best path forward.

Two months later, on June 6, Robert Kennedy was assassinated. Kennedy had decided to run for president after Lyndon B. Johnson told Americans he would not seek another term. Kennedy was intimately involved with the Civil Rights Movement and had been seen as one of the few political leaders who could bring Americans together and begin to heal the wound that King's death had left.

More sadness and disillusion came at the Democratic National Convention held in Chicago in August. Protesters against the Vietnam War were met with National Guard. Delegates were forced to make their way through police lines. Eventually, Democrats nominated Hubert Humphrey as their candidate. He had a stellar record of activism and social justice and had been instrumental in getting the 1964 Civil Rights Act passed in the Senate. He lost to Richard Nixon.

This one turbulent year brought many Americans out of their complacency and left others wondering whether the United States was on the verge of another civil war. Gains were made in education, housing, and wages for many who experienced systemic racism. While there was grief, there was also a commitment to keep the flame alive and ensure that the work of Martin Luther King Jr. continued. Conservative Americans cried out for "law and order" to be restored and expected Richard Nixon to implement strict measures to bring the protesters in line.

Disappointing Accounting

In the fifty years that have passed, the social justice movements and ideals that inspired people to change have become historic relics rather than functional principals. And the change that had been hoped for and promised, and for which lives had been given in sacrifice, does not seem to have manifested itself.

As I listened to that interview with Harry Belafonte, I remembered my own enthusiastic embrace of social justice movements and how committed I felt at the time to ensuring equality and opportunity. I remember my patriotism being awakened as I joined people in the streets calling their elected representatives to task for keeping the war going. I marched with church members in protest of redlining. I volunteered with inner-city youth in an attempt to bridge the racial divide. I voted in every election and assisted others to exercise their right to vote.

But today, as I reflect on what has transpired since 1968, I find myself wondering why that wasn't sufficient. Why haven't we succeeded in learning to love each other? Why did we lose the war on drugs and poverty, and fail to bring the promise of America to all Americans?

Harry Belafonte pulls no punches: "We [African Americans] have been lynched. We have been murdered. And if you look around, never before in my 91 years of history as an American, have I ever seen the nation more racially divisive that it is at this very moment, including the days of the Ku Klux Klan and the segregation laws of the South."

Holding Myself Accountable

When I take myself to task, I realize that I became an armchair liberal who donated to causes I thought were addressing the issues instead of marching and holding people in power accountable. Based on results, this passive approach has not succeeded in shifting the power structure from exclusive control by the few to an inclusive model.

It was not until the last election that Americans once again took to the streets in protest in large numbers. Since January 2017, energetic and coordinated protests have reemerged addressing many of the same themes that were present in 1968: inequity between genders, inequality in work and pay, overt segregation, and systemic imprisonment and slaughter of Black men.

Raising Our Voices Once Again

Men and women of all ages are once again making their voices heard in support of change. We are utilizing strategies that fifty years ago moved our government to rewrite laws and fund programs to bring opportunity and level the playing field. In addition, the voices of young people are calling their elders to action demanding that we protect them and keep them safe in our schools.

Perhaps this is a cycle. Perhaps there really is a continuum and we are at one end and beginning the return to the middle. If such a theory holds true, this return journey will see some gains made, some wrongs righted, and new ideas implemented to address long-standing inequities. As Belafonte says in the closing moments of the interview, "The baton has been passed."

GATES

Originally published February 3, 2019

ALMOST EVERY DAY, I DRIVE by a corner property that has a gate on it. The gate has two large swinging arms, each with five horizontal bars held together with five vertical bars, in the shape "I – W – I." Two heavy posts support these gates at both ends, and the gates themselves are held closed in the middle by a sturdy, heavy-linked chain and padlock. Nothing is going to get past this gate without effort, a key, or going over or under. It is an excellent example of what a gate should be.

Except that it stands alone. Literally by itself. It is as if it were placed there as a monument instead of a working tool.

I am intrigued by this freestanding symbol. What is it keeping out? What is it keeping in? Why does it stand alone? Did fences at one time extend in either direction? Is the gate aware that it is alone?

Follow the Metaphor

This may be a bit of a stretch, but see if you can follow me. My gate is a lot like growing old in the United States. Aging, which once served a clearly defined purpose and worked in concert with other elements in society, now stands alone and is a separate developmental stage. Without context, aging becomes an object to be viewed but not interacted with. It evokes stories, memories, and past glories, but it has a limited utility and can be easily overlooked. Sometimes aging just gets in the way, but it would take too much effort to do something about it. Besides, growing old isn't hurting anything. It has become something that has faded into the background and only occasionally comes into focus.

There are many gates in my life. Some I have spent years erecting. They are well adorned and have fabulous locking mechanisms, and some haven't been opened in a long time. They keep some things in and they keep others out. At least that is what I choose to believe.

But now I am wondering. How many of my gates are like the one in my neighborhood? Have I worked hard enough to remove the fencing that once kept my ego in check or my fears at bay, only to have this last vestige of a barrier remain? Do I find myself standing unconsciously in front of the hasp, unable to remember where I put the key, feeling more and more frustrated, and totally oblivious to the solution that is evident to all others—to just walk around the gate?

Or, worse, do I defend the gate? Do I find ways to strengthen it and create more barriers to further keep at bay whatever I put that gate up against in the first place? Do I maintain the gate for a reason no longer remembered, merely because the gate is tradition, or habit, or no longer part of my consciousness?

I bump into gates I have erected every day. Gates that seem insurmountable, sturdy and forever locked. Gates of worry and fear that I am not good enough or smart enough. That I don't have enough money set aside for my old age. That I will be alone and forgotten. Gates of sadness and grief that keep my heart safe and separate, or so I believe. Gates of memories that stem the flood of tears unless I risk all and leave them open.

And I am not alone in erecting these gates. I listen to politicians arguing about the necessity of building walls and insisting that they are essential for our survival. I look around at the communities in my state and see all kinds of folks erecting barriers designed to limit access. I see members of my community huddling together in self-defined groups, unsure whether they should create gates to let some in or keep some out.

The Irony

The irony of the gate that I drive by almost every day is that it neither keeps things in nor keeps things out. It stands alone, impotent. It is an object of curiosity, since it has no functional purpose. I suspect that many of the gates currently under discussion are just that—objects of curiosity with no functional purpose. Distractions that are designed to take our minds off our feelings of vulnerability and insecurity.

My goal is to pay attention to my gates, to see whether they serve a purpose that is aligned with who I am now. It is one of the gifts of growing older that I can reflect on thoughts, beliefs, and habits that have functioned to hold things in, keep things out, or just slow the intensity and flow of ideas and feelings. This is a worthy endeavor at my stage of life. If my gates no longer serve a purpose, I vow to open them or tear them down.

VALUING OURSELVES AS WE GROW OLDER

Some Additional Thoughts

I have recently been going through things and giving away items that no longer are bringing me joy, as Marie Kondo espouses. This effort has been challenging because many of the items carry with them an emotional legacy tied to memories of people, events, and stories shared with me over the years. They represent a legacy from my family to me. This legacy carries with it a sense of duty and obligation to preserve these objects out of respect for the person who acquired them originally and what they have meant.

Legacies are commonly thought of as relating to things (such as money and objects). I encourage you to expand your definition to include values. A legacy of values includes those values that guide you in making decisions about the quality of life you desire as you age. Values such as tolerance, compassion, and kindness influence how you interact with others. Values such as hard work, keeping a promise, and speaking truthfully influence how you are perceived by others. These are just a few values that are worth cultivating, sharing, and, most important, communicating with the generations that follow.

THIS WEEK IN HISTORY

Originally published February 9, 2020

THERE ARE MOMENTS WHEN I am deeply aware that I am participating in something much larger than my own life sphere. These moments sometimes have great majesty and other times feel deeply personal and yet are shared by others. The birth of a child is one such shared event. Politics is another. This past week was one of those weeks that contains more than the seed of historical importance. But as dramatic as it has been for me and other Americans, does it have the gravitas necessary to become something other than a footnote in history?

Here are some other things than happened on February 5 over the centuries:

1. Roger Williams, founder of Rhode Island, arrived in America (1651).
2. John and Charles Wesley arrived in Georgia and brought Methodism with them (1736).

3. France recognized United States of America and signed the Treaty of Alliance (1778).
4. In Philadelphia, the first motion picture was shown to a theater audience (1870).
5. Southern Pacific Railway completed the "Southern Route" from New Orleans to Los Angeles (1883).
6. The Mexican Constitution was proclaimed (1917).
7. Hank Aaron was born (1934).
8. Franklin D. Roosevelt announced a plan to expand the Supreme Court to fifteen justices (1937).
9. Dwight D. Eisenhower became commander of Allied Forces in North Africa (1943).
10. King George VI died, and Elizabeth II became queen (1952).
11. Nelson Mandela was released from prison (1990).
12. Donald J. Trump, impeached president, was acquitted by the U.S. Senate (2020).

Eavesdropping

What strange alignment of the stars, what karmic convolutions, what random chances caused these events to happen on this day in history? What did John and Charles Wesley discuss as they walked the streets of Savannah, Georgia? What kinds of curious folks came to that theater in Philly to see moving pictures? Were Mr. and Mrs. Aaron pleased with their newborn son, or were they afraid that his future would be bleak? What was FDR thinking when he tried to pack the Court? Did Lilibet have any notion of what her reign would encompass or how she would navigate the tempestuous waters created by twentieth-century paparazzi?

Lincoln famously penned that the "world will little note nor long remember" his remarks on that Thursday afternoon in November 1863 in Gettysburg, Pennsylvania. He modestly suggested that the sacrifices made in battle would have a far greater impact than his words; yet it seems the opposite is true. Unlike Lincoln's remarks, the rhetoric of the past week during the impeachment of the forty-fifth president may be preserved for eternity, but its impact might have already passed.

Real Life Happens at All Levels

History seems to record events of the powerful, the influential, the evil, and only occasionally the mundane. But life is happening at all levels. Acts of courage happened this week not only on the Senate floor, but also in homes around the world where individuals, families, and groups took a stand against hatred and intolerance.

Sacrifices were made with little or no thought as to possible loss or gain for the individual making the sacrifice and in the hope that such actions would result in someone feeling less alone, not so hungry, less pained, freer, and safer. People slowed and stopped to allow pedestrians and ducks to cross the road and did so without swearing or honking a horn.

Kind words, an occasional hug, and jokes were shared, resulting in others feeling seen, appreciated, and joyful. None of these acts will be recorded for posterity, yet they are at the foundation of our society and culture.

Useful Repetition

These legacies of values are typically not explicit. They are simply patterns that are repeated because there is utility in them. Benefits are experienced without fanfare and traditions are reinforced because they help us draw closer together and find common ground rather than difference. And we are better for having done so.

There are valid reasons for elders to be the keepers of these traditions. Having made it through hard times as well as periods of contentment, many older Americans can compare what we are going through today with other, possibly more harrowing, times.

VALUING OURSELVES AS WE GROW OLDER

Elders have acquired the knowledge that it may be easy to get caught up in the winds of change and lose hope. Because they survived these experiences, elders may have a deeper understanding of how important it is to stay the course and gather strength from each other.

Testing Your Values

What are your values? Have you had them tested? Could *you* speak truth to power? Can you find space in your heart to forgive? Can you look at yourself in the mirror and see worth and value?

Hank Aaron made history not only because of his prowess on the baseball field, but also because of his commitment to civil rights. Nelson Mandela stayed true to his conviction that apartheid was wrong and inspired his fellow South Africans to find ways to heal the wounds created by that system. Queen Elizabeth remains the undisputed head of her family, in spite of its dysfunction and discontent. Dwight D. Eisenhower stepped up to the challenge of taming mighty egos and aligning them with the larger purpose of eradicating the evil that was the Nazi war machine. Franklin D. Roosevelt rebounded from his unsuccessful yet unbridled attempt to pack the court and led the country out of the darkness that was the Great Depression. Roger Williams held true to his values of independence and separation of church and state, and followed his conscience even at the peril of exile. John Wesley lived to the ripe old age of eighty-seven and, though he returned to England, he left behind an indelible legacy of sacred hymns and psalms still sung by Methodists today.

We are in need of legacy right now. Using our values to guide us in these challenging times is essential. Each of us has a legacy of values worth curating. Taking time to explore, discuss, and cultivate these values and share them with family members and your larger community is fundamentally necessary if we are to find our way through this current darkness.

STAYING CONNECTED IN OUR SEPARATENESS

Originally published June 7, 2020

WE MUST GET BETTER AT staying connected in our separateness. The events of the past few weeks have numbed me in some ways and in other ways have launched me into action. I sit alone in my home watching evening news trying to make sense of the ever-increasing numbers of assaults on normalcy and hope for a change in the ways we live and work together.

It is impossible to not be questioning what horrible terrible thing will happen next, when in truth, all these things have been going on for decades, many just under the surface and others blatant in their execution, successfully ignored by some or enabled by others. I recall the scene in Casablanca as Bogie and Claude Rains conduct business as usual, knowing that things are changing but not wanting to admit that they will need to change also.

Reminders of Our Vulnerability

The murder of George Floyd, loss of life due to COVID-19, and the collapse of our democracy are frightening reminders of our vulnerability. Pressure, fear, and constrained movements because of the virus have paused our routines and required changes in how we interact on every level. Some of these changes are exhausting. Some have brought out righteous indignation in me that was probably always there but now is freely shared. This information is frequently not appreciated by the receiving parties, who now eagerly and more energetically share their opposing perspectives with me. I find myself impatient and irritable, with little relief from either state.

Descriptors

I am a straight, White, aging, adult female. All those descriptors carry meaning and potency far beyond how I was taught to think of myself. Each of these adjectives separates me from the collective sense of "humanness" I yearn to connect with. Still, individuality lifts us up, and claiming one's identity is an essential step in cultural and biologic development, at least in our industrialized, Western country.

My preference would be to drop all descriptors and just exist in mutual adoration and acceptance. This wish is naive and does not begin to address the generational trauma experienced by those who look different, act differently, speak differently, or do not worship the same God or gods that I do and who have been singled out for these very differences. The concept of "other" seems to be hardwired into our limbic systems, resulting in the neurological "fight-flight-freeze" response when we identify an "other" as a threat. How do we overcome biology? How do we find ways to soothe and calm the response so that we can connect in our humanness?

Empathy or Compassion?

I share the pain of those who are marginalized, although I do not bear their pain. It is much easier to acknowledge someone's suffering than change the conditions that caused that suffering. I suspect that there are many who are capable of understanding someone else's plight but have no insight or inclination to go the next step and see what can be done about alleviating that person's suffering.

As a result, I believe I have a greater responsibility to my fellow beings to take actions that provide comfort and care for those who are hurting and to confront those who have caused the hurt. White privilege has been called out for centuries by those who have been oppressed by it. Today, it is being explored by those who have it. I suspect it will be a while before change is seen in the behaviors of many of us, since our motivation to confront our transgressions is still relatively low. It is here that the COVID-19 may be the great leveler.

A straight, privileged White male who writes opinion columns for a respected newspaper suggested, albeit quite awkwardly, that the pandemic had created circumstances similar to the limitations felt by marginalized people in terms of having to watch where he goes, what he must wear, and how he is perceived. I say awkward because this minor inconvenience is nothing like the conditions in which so many Americans live and work, yet he was seeking to bridge the divide.

Measurable Change

What will accomplish this? In my time on this planet, truly successful and measurable change has come about through government enacting laws and regulations that force people to change behavior. For example, environmental laws have resulted in behavioral changes, with people separating paper from plastic and manufacturers improving their machinery and systems for better air and water quality. Health and safety laws have been passed to ensure that people wear seat belts, drinking water be tested, pharmaceuticals' side effects be made known, and food labels list ingredients—all measures that benefit our health. There are other examples, of course. And still, these are not sufficient to change underlying beliefs and strongly held prejudices that people seem reluctant to give up.

I would like to believe all people are capable of sustained change. Sadly, this has not been my experience. So I stand for compassion and tolerance. These two values appear in every faith and most founding documents of democracies on this planet. They are the "brown gabardine suit" of values—not flashy, but trustworthy and dependable. I have seen people change their behaviors when they have been on the receiving end of compassionate acts or have had sustained contact and interaction with individuals who are different. If only there were opportunities for such experiences to happen for all of us.

PERSONAL VALUES

Originally published August 2, 2020

I HAVE BEEN INTERESTED IN human values since my twenties. The idealism of my stage of development along with the changes happening in society in the late 1960s brought home to me just how key values are in my life. I have consciously and unconsciously lived a values-driven life. And so it is no surprise to me that I am once again seeking to understand the role that values play as I transition from being a working psychologist to being a writer who used to be a psychologist.

The values of my early childhood were steeped in White, Protestant, middle-class terms: patriotism, loyalty, duty, punctuality, cleanliness, and obedience, to list a few. This status quo was rocked by the Civil Rights Movement, the women's liberation movement, and the antiwar movement. Each of these movements arose from values that paralleled the ones I had been taught, but from a different perspective.

Events That Shaped Me

I have never felt more patriotic than when I joined thousands of other antiwar protesters at the Democratic Convention in 1968 in Chicago or when I rode a bus to Washington, D.C., for the March on Washington. I was passionate about engaging in political action that was directed at making my country better.

I have never felt a stronger sense of belonging than when I shared my fears and vulnerabilities in women's consciousness-raising groups, or sang "We Shall Overcome" while protesting segregated schools with African Americans. I learned that taking a stand wasn't always successful in the short term, but every attempt at change furthered the cause.

I learned the benefits of charitable giving by collecting pennies for UNICEF and visiting housebound members of my church to share flowers and conversation with them. These acts were reinforced by the feelings of satisfaction and happiness I experienced in doing them.

Values Motivate

Values are multidimensional, having powerful motivational properties. They can inspire us to take action above and beyond the call of duty—to make sacrifices, including giving our very lives, when we believe in something greater than our small selves. There is no end to the inspirational stories of sacrifices human beings have made to help strangers in times of war or disaster.

Values can also be fear-based. If I believe I am not enough, or I am unlovable, or I do not have enough to survive, I might claim that values such as revenge, blame, or manipulation give me the right to do or have something because these values will level a playing field or restore my reputation or good name.

Abraham Maslow

Back in the late 1960s, Abraham Maslow studied values as a way of understanding what motivated people to strive to grow. His insights have been used by psychologists and businesses in the intervening decades to help develop leaders who make values-driven decisions. Maslow's hierarchy of needs sets out basic tenets required to grow and develop based not only on genetics and circumstance but also on acquisition of skills and attitudes that allow for each of us to develop to our true potential.

For example, it is virtually impossible for someone to flourish if their basic needs for food, clothing, and shelter are at risk (the first two levels in Maslow's hierarchy). We see this happening now with the unexpected economic consequences of the pandemic. Too many humans have a tenuous grip on secure housing, food, and safety. Protections in place since the New Deal have been whittled away, and now many older adults who have relied on subsidized housing to augment their Social Security are on the verge of homelessness. Remaining confined to these levels causes people to experience intense anxiety, chronic depression, and consequently poor health.

Belonging

Having a sense of security that comes from belonging and being loved is a key need if we are to develop. But having our needs for belonging and love met does not guarantee enlightenment; in fact, it is all too easy to turn these needs to the purposes of blind loyalty and harmful and exclusive gangs. The current president understands this tendency all too well and he has used his understanding to create a deeply divisive attachment to his MAGA (Make America Great Again) base. Finding and belonging to something that makes you feel good about yourself can range from being benign (for example, belonging to a fraternity or social service organization) to cultish, such as with members of the Ku Klux Klan or neo-Nazis.

The next level of development in Maslow's hierarchy contains many societal reinforcements. These include a sense of accomplishment, prestige, status, and acknowledgment by others of what you have done. Many older adults, especially those who are no longer finding ways to contribute to their communities through working, volunteering, mentoring, or sharing their wisdom, find themselves becoming invisible. I have worked with older adults who are phenomenally accomplished but are now considered to be stupid, uneducated, or infantile because of the ignorance or ageism of those who are interacting with these adults.

Self-Actualization

The final level of Maslow's pyramid is self-actualization. When Maslow did his initial research, he didn't find many folks who had gotten this far in their development. Now, more than a half-century later, with the emergence of neuroplasticity and the popularity of mindfulness and wellness practices, more and more people are finding their true potential and tapping into wells of creativity.

And what better time for all humanity? We are faced with a plethora of challenges that are proving over-whelming for those who have not been able to move through these levels. A return to tribalism and a systematic destruction of institutions founded on strong values of helping others are forcing many of us to rethink our values. This is a worthwhile practice.

Values as a Decision-Making Tool

If you believe that personal mastery involves overcoming or eliminating fear-based beliefs, then you can understand why it is important to be able to use values as a decision-making tool. When we are out of alignment with what is important to us, we often are frozen in inaction and experience inner conflict and distress.

We are living in times when much is out of alignment. We cannot speak to others if we differ because we cannot find common ground. Finding common ground can be done by exploring what values are shared. From shared values can come shared decision-making instead of blame. And from there, we can find our way out of this mess.

ONCE UPON A TIME . . .

Originally published September 20, 2020

GATHER ROUND, MY DEAR ONES! Come sit at my feet. Now, remember to keep your hands to yourself and pay attention! I am going to tell you a story of a time long, long ago when things were very different. What? You don't believe me? You think I am making this up? Well, my dear ones, just be patient. Listen closely, for you may find something very special in this tale about *you*!

Down the road, not more than a half-day's walk, there once was an ancient wood. This forest was magical in every way. The trees were the most majestic of any trees found anywhere. They rose so high the clouds would nestle among them and join in the songs that were sung when the wind would blow. The forest floor was the softest and most fertile, with mushrooms and ferns, and colonies of small creatures that would eat the dying things and turn them into fertile soil. When you entered the forest, the quiet would gently surround you and invite you to hold your breath until your heart and soul discovered the ancient rhythm that set everything in motion. Then you would exhale, long and deep. Releasing all the tension, fear, and worry that you had unknowingly been carrying outside the wood.

For first-time visitors, finding their way through the wood could be confusing. This was because they used only their eyes and ears to locate the paths. Eyes and ears worked well outside the wood. One glance could identify friend or foe. Sounds could be paid attention to or ignored. But in the wood, there were no familiar ways of identifying friend or foe, so the eyes alone lost focus. And ears that had been trained to pick out whiny voices, or complaining voices, or critical voices were useless when all sounds were harmonious.

It takes a while to learn the secrets of the wood. Do you want to learn some of the secrets, my dear ones?

The first secret (and truth be told, it is really not a secret at all!) is that you need to learn to be quiet. I don't mean quiet like holding your tongue or not talking. No, I mean being quiet inside. So quiet that you can hear your heart beating. So quiet that you can hear the blood pulsing through your veins. So quiet that you can hear your very thoughts as they pass through your awareness.

The second secret is that each and every thing has its own rhythm. Once you have discovered your rhythm, you can learn to speed it up or slow it down. Once you have discovered how to do that, you can match your rhythm to the rhythms of others. That is when you find out what it means to be truly alive. In the wood, you can learn the rhythm of the seasons, the rhythm of birth and death cycles, and the rhythm of ancient time. This, my dear ones, is truly profound, for we are nothing more than a pause between beats in this most ancient of settings.

One more secret (but just this last one because I don't want you to become overwhelmed) is that all of us, within and without the forest, play a role in each other's cycles and rhythms. We don't always know what that role is, which can be frustrating or confusing. It requires that we listen with our forest ears, not our outside-the-forest ears. It requires that we see with our forest eyes, just slightly unfocused, so we can see beyond the edges of things

I know, I have digressed, but it is important that you understand that just going into the wood will not guarantee that you actually make your way through it. And what is on the other side of the wood is so magnificent and so wonderful that you will want to make your way through. Some of you, my dear ones, will never make it through the wood. Some of you will become lost. I know that can be scary. But it is something you all need to understand.

Some of you, though, will learn the secrets of the wood. You will find the paths that will take you to the cool water rushing over the rocks in the streams and rivers. You will find the quiet pools where the fish sleep until they are ready to return to the moving water. You will find the plumpest berries and the sweetest fruits growing on the bushes and trees in different parts of the forest. And, if you are lucky, you will come upon the glade where the fauns are born.

Others of you will find your way to the cliffs and, looking up, will see the eagles soaring overhead. If you enter the wood at dusk, you will feel the wood coming alive, and hear the hooting of the owls and the antiphonal response of the loons on the lake.

It is so easy to fall under the spell of the wood with all its beauty. But there is another side to the wood. There are plants that look inviting but are poisonous. They send mixed messages, and you only learn the consequences after you have come into contact with them. There are pools of water that look inviting, but if you jump in without checking first, you will be boiled alive, for the water's temperature is too hot for people. Other pools will offer the thirsty traveler relief, until you take that first swallow and find it is all salty and undrinkable.

So, my dears, what do you make of this wood? Is it a place to explore, or are you afraid to enter? Can you imagine what it would be like if we didn't have such a magnificent place? How else would we learn the secrets of listening with our heart and pausing long enough to match our rhythm to the rest of the world?

When I was your age, I would go there all the time. I learned to listen with my heart. I saw the eagles and found the faun's birthing nest. I heard the loons at sunset. When I am gone, dear ones, so will the connection to the wood be gone. I am so very sad you will never be able to walk in such a wonderful place.

No, dear ones. Please forgive me! I meant to tell you a pleasing fairy tale, not get you all upset. Still, perhaps there is value in being upset. There still is time, just not much. And we have many challenges ahead. Maybe we can use the secrets of the wood to bring us through.

Resources

I have cited a number of different websites throughout this book. Should you wish to go to the original source, here are the websites. Listed first is the Title, followed by the key word or individual linked to the website (in italics), followed by the web address.

Giving and Receiving, *The Elders*,
    theelders.org 12

Because I Could Not Stop for Death, *POLST*,
    polst.org 29

Generation Gaps *"meme-to-merch"*
    nytimes.com/2019/10/29/style/ok-boomer.html, ...43

Generation Gaps, *Taylor Lorenz*, "'OK Boomer' Marks End of Friendly Generational Relations," October 29, 2019, nytimes.com/2019/10/29/style/ok-boomer.html 43

Left Behind, *Living/Dying Project*,
    livingdying.org/conscious-dying/............................53

To Everything There Is A Season, *Turn, Turn, Turn,*
youtube.com/watch?v=pKP4cfU28vM 73

The Importance of Leaving A Legacy of Values, *Carolina Herrera, Global Brand Ambassador,*
nytimes.com/2018/02/09/fashion/carolina-herrera-final-show-new-york-fashion-week.html?hpw&rref=fashion&action=click&pgtype=Homepage&module=well-region&region=bottom-well&WT.nav=bottom-well" 91

Passing the Baton, *Harry Belafonte,*
pbs.org/newshour/show/harry-belafonte-to-realize-martin-luther-king-jr-s-dream-white-america-needs-to-change-course 103

Staying Connected in Our Separateness, *Casablanca,*
youtube.com/watch?v=qmywwiZth5E 121

Five Pillars of Aging,
fivepillarsofaging.com 141

ABOUT THE AUTHOR

MARY L. FLETT, PHD is an author who used to be a psychologist. In addition to writing, she is a nationally-recognized speaker and has led seminars on aging across the country. In this first book in her series, *Aging with Finesse*, she shares her insights and wisdom gleaned from over 30 years of working with elders as a psychologist, and a lifetime of mentoring by older friends and relatives. She is the Executive Director of the Center for Aging and Values and, in her spare time, runs Five Pillars of Aging, offering online and in-person programs on how to age better and age well.

www.ingramcontent.com/pod-product-compliance
Lightning Source LLC
Chambersburg PA
CBHW071244070526
44583CB00017B/2325